Baseball
LEGENDS

D1193771

PUBLICATIONS INTERNATIONAL, LTD.

CONTENTS

100 BASEBALL GREATS

◆　　　◆　　　◆

THE HISTORY OF BASEBALL lies in the history of its players—from Ty Cobb's relentless pursuit of excellence to Babe Ruth's zestful pursuit of, well, just about everything. Throughout baseball's colorful history, there have been players with considerable statistical totals, and there have been those whose leadership and strength of character led their teams to victory. Above all of these, some players were blessed with both attributes. These are the players whose lives have become synonymous with the game—the superstars, the immortals. *Baseball Legends* pays tribute to 100 of these great men.

Willie Mays once said: "It isn't hard to be good from time to time in sports.

What's hard is to be good every day." The players included in this book were good just about every day. Consider Lou Gehrig, with his 2,130 consecutive games played and a lifetime batting average of .340. Or Hank Aaron and his 755 home runs. Or Christy Mathewson and his 373 victories on the mound. These feats are not merely record-book accomplishments, but are testaments to the tenacity and enthusiasm these gifted players brought to the game.

The pages of *Baseball Legends* bring offensive greats such as Ted Williams and Harmon Killebrew to the plate and pitching legends such as Lefty Grove and Walter Johnson to the mound. Step into the Yankee dynasty of the '50s with Joe DiMaggio and Yogi Berra, and revisit the stars of the crosstown Brooklyn Dodgers, Jackie Robinson and Duke Snider. *Baseball Legends* includes all the names that have made baseball America's national pastime.

HANK AARON

OUTFIELDER

MILWAUKEE BRAVES 1954-1965
ATLANTA BRAVES 1966-1974
MILWAUKEE BREWERS 1975-1976

◆　　　◆　　　◆

ON APRIL 23, 1954, Hank Aaron hit his first of 755 major-league home runs, more than any player in history.

Henry Louis Aaron (born in 1934) grew up one of eight children in Mobile, Alabama. He learned baseball by hitting bottle caps with a broomstick, and started playing semipro ball in Mobile at age 16. By 1951, the Indianapolis Clowns of the Negro Leagues signed him as a shortstop. He was a cross-handed hitter for awhile, but switched to a conventional grip on a scout's advice and hit two home runs in his first game with the new grip.

The Braves signed Aaron in 1952 and sent him to Eau Clair of the Northwest League, where he batted .336. In 1953, he was one of three players to integrate the South Atlantic League. He led the circuit with a .362 average, 125 RBI, and 115 runs scored. Bobby Thomson, the Braves left fielder, broke his ankle early in 1954, and Hank inherited the job in Milwaukee.

"I don't want them to forget Ruth. I just want them to remember me."
—HANK AARON LATE IN THE 1973 SEASON

Aaron endured the bigotry and segregation of the major leagues at that time with poise and silence. In his early years in the majors, he was an enigma to most players and fans. He let his bat do the talking for many years, and only gradually did his image evolve from that of a hitting machine to an intelligent, forceful man who could set seemingly impossible goals and achieve them.

Hank had an all-around game that was second to none. He became one of the top outfielders in the game after coming up as an infielder. He was consistent and careful and deadly. His quick wrists were the stuff of legend. He led the NL with a .328 batting average in 1956. In 1957, he won the National League MVP Award with a .328 batting average, 44 home runs, and 132 RBI. The Braves won the pennant that year, and then went on to defeat a powerful Yankee team in the World Series. Hank hit .393 in the seven games with three home runs. Although the Braves remained a strong team for many years, it was to be Aaron's only world title. The Yankees repaid the Braves in the 1958 Series, although Aaron hit .333 in the Series.

The Braves moved to Atlanta from Milwaukee in 1966, and Aaron, who had been succeeding for years in one of the very worst parks for hitters in baseball, was granted a reprieve; Fulton County Stadium proved to be a great hitter's park. He hit 245 home runs after turning 35 years old, a record. He hit .357 with three homers in the 1969 NLCS, the only other postseason appearance of his long career.

On April 8, 1974, Aaron broke Babe Ruth's lifetime home run record. Racism and fans' misguided reverence for the Babe added to the difficulty of that monumental task. Always a quiet, serious professional, Henry withstood the burden and scrutiny of an all-out media assault with cool and restraint. "Thank God it's over," he said after the record-breaking game.

Aaron won a record eight total-bases titles, en route to the all-time record of 6,856 total bases. He slugged over .500 18 times and batted over .300 14 times. He drove in 100 runs in 13 consecutive seasons and 15 times in all, finishing his career with an all-time best 2,297 runs batted in. Pitcher Curt Simmons said, "Throwing a fastball by Henry Aaron is like trying to sneak the sun past a rooster." Aaron was inducted into the Hall of Fame in 1982.

MAJOR LEAGUE TOTALS									
BA	G	AB	R	H	2B	3B	HR	RBI	SB
.305	3,298	12,364	2,174	3,771	624	98	755	2,297	240

GROVER ALEXANDER

P I T C H E R

PHILADELPHIA PHILLIES 1911-1917; 1930
CHICAGO CUBS 1918-1926
ST. LOUIS CARDINALS 1926-1929

◆　　　◆　　　◆

G ROVER CLEVELAND ALEXANDER (1887-1950) paced the New York State League at age 23 with 29 wins in 1910, and Syracuse sold him to the Philadelphia Phillies for $750.

With the acquisition of Alexander, the Phillies almost instantly became a contender. In 1911, "Pete" won 28 games, a modern rookie record, and also set National League rookie marks for strikeouts and shutouts.

Alexander's seven years in Philadelphia were the most successful and probably the happiest of his life. In 1915, his 31 wins spearheaded the Phillies to their only pennant before 1950. The following season, he scored a personal-high 33 victories and notched an all-time record 16 shutouts. When he won 30 again in 1917, he became the last pitcher to be a 30-game winner in two consecutive seasons, let alone three.

"Less than a foot made the difference between a hero and a bum."
—GROVER ALEXANDER, ON TONY LAZZERI'S LONG FOUL THE PITCH BEFORE STRIKING OUT IN THE 1926 WORLD SERIES

Serving on the front in World War I, Alexander lost the hearing in one ear as a result of a shelling and also began experiencing the first symptoms of epilepsy. Between the illness and the shell shock he had suffered, he came to rely more and more on alcohol for solace.

Upon his return from overseas, Alexander rejoined the Cubs and had several outstanding years with Chicago. Waived to the Cardinals in early 1926, now known as "Old Pete," he came to St. Louis with a chronic sore arm and a reputation for no longer being able to keep his drinking under control.

In the 1926 World Series against the Yankees, however, Alexander won both the second and sixth games in a starting role. But in Game 7, when New York loaded the bases in the seventh inning with two out, Alexander was called out of the bullpen to protect a 3-2 St. Louis lead. Despite nursing a monumental hangover, he proceeded to fan rookie sensation Tony Lazzeri on four pitches. Pete then set down the vaunted New Yorkers in the final two innings without surrendering a hit.

Alexander won 21 games in 1927, the ninth and last time he reached the magic circle. His career ended in 1930, and he was named to the Hall of Fame in 1938.

MAJOR LEAGUE TOTALS									
W	L	ERA	G	CG	IP	H	ER	BB	SO
373	208	2.56	696	438	5,189.1	4,868	1,474	953	2,199

CAP ANSON

FIRST BASEMAN

ROCKFORD FOREST CITYS 1871
PHILADELPHIA ATHLETICS 1872-1875
CHICAGO WHITE STOCKINGS 1876-1897

MANAGER

PHILADELPHIA ATHLETICS 1875
CHICAGO WHITE STOCKINGS 1879-1897
NEW YORK GIANTS 1898
1,292-945

◆   ◆   ◆

ADRIAN CONSTANTINE ANSON (1852-1922) was perhaps the most influential on-field figure of baseball's early years. Not only was he an outstanding player, but he was an innovative and fiery manager as well.

Anson was one of the very few early stars whose father encouraged him to pursue a career in pro baseball. The elder Anson even wrote a letter to the Chicago team in 1869 recommending his son. The letter was ignored, but Adrian signed in

1871 with Rockford in the National Association. The next season he joined the Philadelphia Athletics and remained with them through 1875. The next year Anson and several teammates jumped to the Chicago White Stockings of the new National League.

Anson collected exactly 3,000 hits, becoming the first to do so. He also was the first manager to institute spring training for players.

A wizard with a bat, Anson batted under .300 only three times in his 27-year career, registering a lifetime .329 mark. He collected exactly 3,000 hits, becoming the first to do so. Cap also led the National League in RBI nine times between 1880 and 1891. Furthermore, he paced the loop twice in batting average. As a player-manager, "Pop" led Chicago to five pennants. He also was the first to institute spring training for players.

Anson was not without flaws, however. His vile on-field language often drew fines from umpires, and he was called "Crybaby" due to his endless complaining. Moreover, Anson believed the major leagues should be the province only of white players. Largely because of his efforts, blacks were barred ("unofficially," of course) from big-league playing fields.

During the 1897 season, Anson lost control of his players, and White Stockings president James Hart demanded that Cap resign as manager. Anson refused, and was fired. After leaving baseball, Anson starred with his family in a vaudeville act. In 1939, Anson was elected to baseball's Hall of Fame.

MAJOR LEAGUE TOTALS									
BA	G	AB	R	H	2B	3B	HR	RBI	SB
.329	2,276	9,108	1,719	3,000	528	124	96	1,715	247

LUIS APARICIO

SHORTSTOP

CHICAGO WHITE SOX 1956-1962; 1968-1970
BALTIMORE ORIOLES 1963-1967
BOSTON RED SOX 1971-1973

◆   ◆   ◆

SHORTSTOP LUIS APARICIO, who patrolled American League infields from 1956 to 1973, was one of the best fielders ever at the position. He teamed with Nellie Fox to form one of the top keystone combinations in baseball history.

Luis Ernesto Aparicio y Montiel was born in 1934 in Maracaibo, Venezuela. His father, Luis Aparicio Sr., was the best shortstop in Venezuela for 25 years. Junior took his father's position on the town team in 1953 and was signed by Chicago the next season. Aparicio's debut with the White Sox was a success. He won the 1956 Rookie of the Year Award by hitting .266 with a league-best 21 stolen bases.

The "Go-Go Sox" finally won the AL flag in 1959, finishing last in home runs but first in steals. All-Stars Aparicio and second baseman Fox led the league at their positions in putouts, assists, and fielding percentage. Fox won the Most Valuable Player Award, and Aparicio was second in the voting. Luis also led the Baltimore Orioles to the 1966 world championship.

Aparicio clearly was born to play shortstop, so much so that he never performed for a single inning at any other position in his 20-year professional career.

Aparicio's 56 steals in 1959 led the league and represented a new level of performance for him. He posted totals of 51, 53, 31, 40, and 57 from 1960 to 1964, and only one rival swiped over 30 bases in that span. He won nine consecutive stolen base titles, something no one else has done. Along with Maury Wills and Lou Brock, Aparicio ushered in the running game of the 1960s.

Aparicio won nine Gold Gloves and led his league in fielding average eight times and assists seven times.

Aparicio's glovework sealed his 1984 Hall of Fame election. He was an unparalleled defensive player. Luis set career shortstop records for the most games (2,581), the most double plays (1,553), and the most assists (8,016). He won nine Gold Gloves and led his league in fielding average eight times and assists seven times.

MAJOR LEAGUE TOTALS									
BA	G	AB	R	H	2B	3B	HR	RBI	SB
.262	2,599	10,230	1,335	2,677	394	92	83	791	506

LUKE APPLING

SHORTSTOP

CHICAGO WHITE SOX 1930-1943; 1945-1950

◆   ◆   ◆

LUKE APPLING never reached the World Series, didn't play flashy defense, and hit only 45 career homers, but he sustained a remarkable level of performance for many years. Appling batted over .300 16 times in a 20-year career and collected 2,749 career hits.

Lucius Benjamin Appling (1907-1991) was purchased in 1930 by the White Sox, for whom he would play his entire career. He became the full-time shortstop in 1933 and won the first of his two batting titles in 1936 with a career-best .388 average. He was named the outstanding major-league shortstop by *The Sporting News*, an honor he also received in 1940 and 1943. Appling also drew nearly 90 walks a season, leading to a career on-base percentage of .396. He once fouled off 19 pitches in a single at bat.

Appling hit .317 in 1937, but a broken leg in 1938 robbed him of some speed and range. In 1940, he lost the batting crown to Joe DiMaggio, .352 to .348. Luke won another title in 1943 with a .328 average, but then went to war, missing the entire 1944 season and most of 1945.

"That's $27.50 and I'm not done yet."

—LUKE APPLING, AFTER FOULING 10 STRAIGHT PITCHES INTO THE STANDS, TO A WHITE SOX CLUB OFFICIAL AFTER BEING DENIED A REQUEST FOR TWO BASEBALLS TO GIVE TO ADMIRING FANS BECAUSE THEY COST $2.75 APIECE

Pushing 40, Appling hit over .300 each year from 1946 to 1949 and made his last All-Star appearance in 1947. He always seemed to have an injury, and his constant moaning led to the nickname "Old Aches and Pains." When his average slipped to just .234 in 1950, he retired after 2,422 games.

Appling set big-league records for shortstops (since broken by Luis Aparicio) in games and double plays, as well as AL marks for putouts, assists, and total chances. Appling, voted into Cooperstown in 1964, remained in baseball as a scout, coach, and manager for many years, and homered in the first Cracker-Jack Old Timers Game, held in 1985.

				MAJOR LEAGUE TOTALS					
AB	G	AB	R	H	2B	3B	HR	RBI	SB
.310	2,422	8,857	1,319	2,749	440	102	45	1,116	179

ERNIE BANKS

SHORTSTOP
FIRST BASEMAN

CHICAGO CUBS 1953-1971

◆　　　◆　　　◆

ERNIE BANKS'S REPUTATION as a goodwill ambassador should not obscure his great playing ability. He was a fine fielder and a power hitter who had an unbridled enthusiasm for baseball.

Born in 1931, Ernest Banks played four sports in high school, but it was his play in a church softball league that induced the semipro Amarillo Colts to sign Ernie at age 17, in 1948. Within two years, he made it to the Kansas City Monarchs, one of the best teams in the Negro Leagues. He played one season before he was drafted into the Army for two years. After his discharge, the Monarchs sold him to the Cubs.

Banks was the everyday shortstop in 1954, hitting .275 with 19 home runs and

79 RBI. In 1955, he batted .295 and clubbed 44 home runs, while setting a major-league record with five grand slams. Banks hit .285 with 43 homers in 1957. He was the first player from a sub-.500 team to be voted the league's Most Valuable Player when he led the league with 47 home runs (the most ever by a shortstop) and 129 RBI in 1958. The following year he became the first player in the NL to win back-to-back MVP Awards. He again led the league in RBI (143) and had 45 homers. He led the NL with 41 homers in 1960.

"Without [Banks] the Cubs would finish in Albuquerque."

—JIMMY DYKES

Banks was a fine shortstop for nine seasons, winning a Gold Glove in 1960. He set a rookie record with 105 double plays in 1954. He was a nine-time All-Star. His move to first base in 1962 was brought on by knee injuries, not defensive shortcomings. He had 37 homers and 104 RBI during the '62 season.

Banks hit more than 40 homers five times, and had more than 100 RBI in eight campaigns. He had more than 80 RBI in 13 seasons. Although the Cubs failed to win a pennant during Ernie's 19-year career, he earned the title "Mr. Cub." He was well known for his love of the game. His credo, "It's a great day for a ball game—let's play two," has become part of the language. He remained a hero in Chicago after his retirement as a player, as he took up a new career in the Cubs' front office. Banks was inducted into the Hall of Fame in 1977.

MAJOR LEAGUE TOTALS									
BA	G	AB	R	H	2B	3B	HR	RBI	SB
.274	2,528	9,421	1,305	2,583	407	90	512	1,636	50

Cool Papa Bell

OUTFIELDER

TEAMS INCLUDE: ST. LOUIS STARS, DETROIT WOLVES, KANSAS CITY MONARCHS, PITTSBURGH CRAWFORDS, CHICAGO AMERICAN GIANTS, HOMESTEAD GRAYS 1922-1946

◆　　　◆　　　◆

NEGRO LEAGUE LEGEND "Cool Papa" Bell was a switch-hitter with tremendous power and amazing speed. Long-time teammate Satchel Paige said Bell could turn out the light and be in bed before the room got dark.

James Thomas Bell (1903-1991) moved at age 17 to St. Louis, where his mother felt he would get a good education. The St. Louis Stars signed him in 1922 as a knuckleball pitcher. Before being switched to the outfield, he earned his nickname by falling asleep before he pitched. He was a "Cool Papa."

The popular Bell remained with the Stars for 10 seasons, but gained his fame with the great Pittsburgh Crawfords and, later, with the Homestead Grays. In 1933, he joined the Crawfords, a team that raided other clubs to acquire future Hall of Famers Satchel Paige, Oscar Charleston, Judy Johnson, and Josh Gibson. Many other fine players toiled for the Crawfords at some time from 1933 to 1936.

"The only comparison I can give is— suppose Willie Mays had never had a chance to play big league? Then I were to come to you and try to tell you about Willie Mays. Now this is the way it is with Cool Papa Bell."

—MONTE IRVIN

Bell joined other Negro Leaguers playing in both the Dominican Republic and in Mexico. Bell was in such demand that he played for 29 summers and 21 winters. He was still hitting .300 at age 48, though fielding was no longer his strong suit. At times, his teams played three games in three towns in one day, traveling by bus.

Bell's lifetime average, by available records, was .338, and he hit .395 in exhibition games against major-leaguers. He once stole over 175 bases in a 200-game season, but as he remembered, "One day I got five hits and stole five bases, but none of that was written down because they didn't bring the score book to the game that day." Happily, the Hall of Fame remembered enough to induct Bell in 1974.

NEGRO LEAGUE STATS*

BA	G	AB	H	2B	3B	HR	SB
.338	919	3,952	1,335	203	68	56	173

*Note: Bell's career stats are incomplete.

JOHNNY BENCH

CATCHER

CINCINNATI REDS 1967-1983

◆ ◆ ◆

JOHNNY BENCH was the best offensive and defensive catcher in baseball for a decade. The first player from the draft to be inducted into the Hall of Fame (in 1989), he ranks among the greatest catchers in baseball history.

Bench hit with enough power to lead the National League in homers twice and in RBI three times. He monopolized the Gold Glove Award from 1968 through 1977. His arm, which would have been an asset in any year, became even more important when artificial turf was giving baserunners an extra step.

Johnny Lee Bench (born in 1947) grew up in Oklahoma City admiring the play of another Okie, Mickey Mantle. Bench was an outstanding high school athlete, and Cincinnati drafted him on the second round of the 1965 draft.

Hitting success is "inner conceit. It's knowing within yourself you can meet any situation."

—JOHNNY BENCH

The Reds promoted Bench in 1968. He was the National League Rookie of the Year with a .275 average, 15 homers, and 82 RBI. He also laid the foundations for a defensive reputation that was to become legendary. He led the '68 NL in putouts and assists, popularizing a one-handed catching method that gave him greater mobility and allowed him to utilize his cannonlike right arm.

Bench won Most Valuable Player Awards in 1970 and '72, leading the Reds to the playoffs both years. In 1970, at age 22, he was the youngest man to ever win the award. He led the league with 45 homers and 148 RBI. His second MVP

Award came two years later in 1972, after batting .270 with 40 home runs and 125 RBI.

Bench and the Reds won consecutive World Series in 1975 and '76, and the Big Red Machine won 210 games during those two seasons. Bench hit .533 in the 1976 World Series, winning the Series MVP Award.

Bench's 327 homers as a catcher were a record when he retired after the 1983 season. He had 20 or more home runs in 11 seasons, drove in more than 100 runs six times, and won 10 consecutive Gold Gloves from 1968 to 1977. During his last three seasons, he played more games at first and third to extend his career. Bench drove in more runs in the 1970s than any other player, 1,013, and was named to 14 All-Star Games.

MAJOR LEAGUE TOTALS

BA	G	AB	R	H	2B	3B	HR	RBI	SB
.267	2,158	7,658	1,091	2,048	381	24	389	1,376	68

YOGI BERRA

CATCHER

NEW YORK YANKEES 1946-1963
NEW YORK METS 1965

◆   ◆   ◆

YOGI BERRA was a mainstay of the most dominating baseball team in history, the New York Yankee team that played from the end of World War II until the early 1960s. He was just the third man to win three Most Valuable Player Awards, and he played in 14 World Series—more than any other player.

Lawrence Peter Berra (born in 1925) grew up in an Italian neighborhood in St. Louis with his buddy Joe Garagiola. He signed with the Yanks in 1943, but soon after joined the Navy. Berra saw action in the Normandy Invasion.

In 1946, Berra was discharged and played for Newark, hitting .314 with 15 homers. That season he was called up to the Yankees, with whom he would star until 1963.

Berra captured the imagination of baseball fans with his malapropisms. "It ain't over till it's over" has become a rally-ing cry for anyone trailing in a game. He was stocky and short, with a broad face and a well-publicized penchant for comic books and a natural quality that fans found amusing and endearing. He was also one of the most dangerous hitters in the Amer-ican League.

Yogi didn't become the Yanks' No. 1 catcher until 1949. In 1950, he batted .322 with 28 homers and 124 RBI. Although his 1951 season wasn't as impressive (a .294 batting average, 27 home runs, and 88 RBI), he won his first MVP Award. His 1952 and 1953 seasons weren't much dif-ferent than his 1954 (a .307 average, 22 homers, 125 RBI) and his 1955 (a .272 average, 27 homers, 108 RBI) seasons, but he won consecutive MVPs in 1954 and '55. It was a tribute to his consistency that his three MVP seasons were not necessarily his best years. He had 90 RBI in nine seasons and 20 homers in 11 seasons.

"It ain't over till it's over."

—Yogi Berra

Berra worked to become a fine defensive catcher and in 1958 fielded a perfect 1.000. He was a wonderful handler of pitchers and a wizard, for a catcher, at the double play. Berra's teams were not stocked like the 1927 Yankees, yet they won five consecutive World Series. Berra owns a host of World Series records and was named an All-Star from 1948 to 1962. He also managed the Yankees and the Mets to pennants. He was inducted into the Hall of Fame in 1972.

MAJOR LEAGUE TOTALS									
BA	G	AB	R	H	2B	3B	HR	RBI	SB
.285	2,120	7,555	1,175	2,150	321	49	358	1,430	30

WADE BOGGS

BOSTON RED SOX 1982-1992
NEW YORK YANKEES 1993-1996

◆   ◆   ◆

N O ONE IN THE 1980s and early 1990s reached base more consistently than Wade Boggs.

Wade Anthony Boggs, born in 1958 in Omaha, was drafted by the Boston Red Sox in 1976. He batted .263 in the New York-Penn League that year, the only time until 1992 that he hit under .300. Lacking power, Wade needed high averages to progress. When he won the 1981 International League batting title, the Red Sox promoted Boggs. When Boggs made the Red Sox in 1982, he played first and third base and batted .349 in 104 games. He won the third baseman's job the next season when Boston jettisoned incumbent Carney Lansford, who had won the American League batting crown the previous season.

From his rookie year through 1989, Boggs's worst average was .325. He won AL batting titles five of his first seven seasons. He produced 200 or more hits seven consecutive times. He was the first player since Stan Musial in 1953 to total 200 or more hits and 100 or more walks in the same season. Boggs, a phenomenally disciplined batter, never swung at the first pitch or at balls out of the strike zone.

From 1983 to 1991, Boggs not only won five AL batting crowns, but he also finished second in the league in batting once and third in the loop twice.

The hard-working Boggs devoted extra time to his defense. He used his good range and excellent reflexes to lead AL third basemen once in putouts and twice in double plays. He won Gold Gloves in 1994 and '95.

Eight times, Boggs hit 40 or more doubles in a season. He paced the American League twice in two-baggers, twice in walks, and twice in runs scored. In 1987, he surprised the league with a career-high 24 homers.

In 1992, Boggs slumped to .259 and seven home runs. That winter, he left Boston to sign with the rival Yankees. He rebounded to bat over .300 each year through 1996, winning his first world championship that fall.

MAJOR LEAGUE TOTALS									
BA	G	AB	R	H	2B	3B	HR	RBI	SB
.333	2,123	8,100	1,367	2,697	518	55	105	905	20

GEORGE BRETT

THIRD BASEMAN
FIRST BASEMAN

KANSAS CITY ROYALS 1973-1993

◆　　　　◆　　　　◆

ONE OF THE TOP PLAYERS during his era and best third basemen of all time, George Brett led the expansion Royals' rise into a championship club on his way to 3,154 base hits.

In 1980, George Howard Brett (born in 1953) came closer to batting .400 than any player since Ted Williams in 1941. Brett was hitting .400 into the final weeks of the 1980 season, and ended the year with a .390 batting average. While he was considered a very good player before then, Brett became a superstar in 1980, winning the AL MVP by adding 24 homers and 118 RBI. He led KC to the ALCS, where the Royals finally defeated the Yankees. The finale was iced by a clutch three-run homer by Brett. Although the Royals lost the World Series to Philadelphia in six games, Brett collected nine hits for a .375 average.

> ## "George Brett could get good wood on an aspirin."
>
> —JIM FREY

Brett is the younger brother of big-league pitcher Ken, who was 83-85 in 14 seasons. The 1975 season gave the first hint of George's ability. He led the AL with 195 hits and 13 triples while batting .308. He won his first batting crown in 1976 (at age 23) with a .333 mark. The Royals won the AL West in just their eighth year of existence, only to lose to the Yankees, a fate that Kansas City would suffer the next two years.

The Royals won their first world championship in 1985 against the Cardinals. That season Brett had 30 homers, 112 RBI, and a .335 average. He had three homers, five RBI, and a .348 average as the Royals came back from a three-games-to-one deficit to beat Toronto in the playoffs. The Royals also rallied from a three-games-to-one deficit to win the Series, with George batting .370.

Brett made headlines in the famous "Pine Tar Incident" on May 24, 1983, when Yankee manager Billy Martin pressured the umpires to disallow a Brett game-winning, two-out home run because of a technicality (pine tar running too far up the bat), calling him out instead. Brett became enraged, KC protested, and the ruling was later overturned. Brett was also the first player to win batting crowns in three different decades, winning the crown in 1976, in 1980, and in 1990 at age 37.

MAJOR LEAGUE TOTALS									
BA	G	AB	R	H	2B	3B	HR	RBI	SB
.305	2,707	10,349	1,583	3,154	665	137	317	1,595	201

DAN BROUTHERS

FIRST BASEMAN

TROY TROJANS 1879-1880
BUFFALO BISONS 1881-1885
DETROIT WOLVERINES 1886-1888
BOSTON BEANEATERS 1889
BOSTON REDS 1890-1891
BROOKLYN BRIDEGROOMS 1892-1893
BALTIMORE ORIOLES 1894-1895
LOUISVILLE COLONELS 1895
PHILADELPHIA PHILLIES 1896
NEW YORK GIANTS 1904

◆   ◆   ◆

DAN BROUTHERS was the greatest hitter of professional baseball's first two decades. He won five batting titles and at one time or another led his league in every major hitting department.

Dennis Joseph Brouthers (1858-1932) reached the National League in 1879. Originally a pitcher, he soon shifted to first base. Back in the NL in 1881 with Buffalo,

Big Dan teamed with Deacon White, Hardy Richardson, and Jack Rowe to form an offensive force labeled "The Big Four." Brouthers led the NL in batting average, slugging average, and on-base percentage in both 1882 and 1883.

Brouthers played on flag-winning teams in three different major leagues.

Financially strapped Buffalo sold the entire Big Four to Detroit in mid-September 1885 for $7,500. NL President Nick Young allowed the deal to stand only if the four did not play against pennant contenders. Due to this ruling, the Big Four missed the last three weeks of the season as all Detroit's remaining games were with teams in the race for the flag.

Playing a full schedule for Detroit in 1886, Brouthers led the league with 11 homers. The following season, his 153 runs scored, 36 doubles, and .426 on-base percentage (all league-leading figures) sparked the Wolverines to their only pennant. When Detroit folded in 1888, Brouthers was awarded to the Boston Beaneaters. The next year, Big Dan won his third batting crown. In 1890 and 1891, Brouthers played for flag-winning Boston clubs in the Players' League and the American Association. He also played with the 1894 champion Orioles.

Brouthers served with a record nine different NL teams, the last being the New York Giants, for whom he played two games in 1904 at age 46. His .342 lifetime average is the eighth best in history, and the best ever for a first baseman. Brouthers was elected to the Hall of Fame in 1945.

MAJOR LEAGUE TOTALS									
BA	G	AB	R	H	2B	3B	HR	RBI	SB
.342	1,673	6,711	1,523	2,296	460	205	106	1,057	235

THREE FINGER BROWN

PITCHER

St. Louis Cardinals 1903
Chicago Cubs 1904-1912; 1916
Cincinnati Reds 1913
St. Louis Terriers 1914
Brooklyn Tip-Tops 1914
Chicago Whales 1915

◆   ◆   ◆

THREE FINGER BROWN was one of a kind. He became a star because of, rather than in spite of, a severe injury.

While on his uncle's farm, seven-year-old Mordecai Peter Centennial Brown (1876-1948) accidentally stuck his right hand under a corn chopper. Before he could retrieve the hand, half of his index finger was torn off, and the thumb and middle finger were also permanently impaired.

The damaged hand hampered Brown whenever he tried to play third base but strangely seemed to work to his advantage when he turned to pitching in his early 20s. Brown found that the unnatural grip he had to employ caused many of his straight pitches to behave like knucklers and imparted an extra dip to his curves.

"To know for sure, I'd have to throw with a normal hand, and I've never tried it."
—THREE FINGER BROWN, WHEN ASKED IF HIS CURVE WAS HELPED BY HIS MISSING INDEX FINGER

Brown joined the Cardinals in 1903. Thinking that his crippled hand would handicap him in the long term, the Cardinals dealt him to the Cubs before the 1904 season. With Chicago, Brown achieved almost instant stardom and became the linchpin of the mound staff.

On June 13, 1905, Brown and Christy Mathewson of the Giants hooked up in one of the greatest pitching duels ever. Brown surrendered just one hit but came out a loser, 1-0, when Mathewson held the

Cubs hitless. From that point through 1909, Brown topped the great Matty on nine consecutive occasions.

With Brown's right arm leading the way, the Cubs won four pennants and two World Series between 1906 and 1910. The second and last title came in 1908 against Detroit and saw Brown win two games and post a perfect 0.00 ERA. Two years earlier, Brown came through the regular season with a 1.04 ERA to set a 20th century NL record.

Used not only as a starting pitcher but also as the Cubs' main stopper, Brown topped the NL in 1911 with 53 mound appearances while compiling a 21-11 record. It was the last of his six consecutive 20-win seasons. Brown died in 1948, one year before he was elected to the Hall of Fame.

MAJOR LEAGUE TOTALS									
W	L	ERA	G	CG	IP	H	ER	BB	SO
239	129	2.06	481	271	3,172.1	2,708	726	673	1,375

ROY CAMPANELLA

CATCHER

NEGRO LEAGUE TEAM
BALTIMORE ELITE GIANTS 1937-1942; 1944-1945
MAJOR LEAGUE TEAM
BROOKLYN DODGERS 1948-1957

◆　　　　◆　　　　◆

ROY CAMPANELLA—along with Jackie Robinson and Don Newcombe—was a pioneering black ballplayer who boosted a Dodger organization that to this day is acknowledged as one of the top teams in baseball history.

Born in Philadelphia, Roy Campanella (1921-1993) as a youngster decided to become a catcher because no one else had signed up for that position in school. He played well enough that in 1937 the 15-year-old backstop was catching on the weekends for the semipro Bacharach Giants. He moved to the Baltimore Elite

Giants, with whom he played most of his career in the Negro Leagues. By the mid-1940s, Campy challenged Josh Gibson as the best catcher in the Negro Leagues.

"From the start, catching appealed to me as a chance to be in the thick of the game continuously."

—ROY CAMPANELLA

Campy was a success from the day he arrived in Brooklyn in mid-1948. The stocky catcher had a rocket for an arm and a powerful bat, and he handled a legendary pitching staff to five pennants in 10 years. Campanella was a prime reason the 1950s Dodgers were the exceptional team in the National League. In 1951, Campanella won the first of three Most Valuable Player Awards. He batted .325 with 33 homers and 108 RBI. His 1953 MVP season was among the best ever recorded by a catcher, as he led the league with 142 RBI, clubbed 41 homers, scored 103 runs, and batted .312.

Campanella chipped a bone in his left hand in spring training in 1954, and he hit only .207 in 111 games that year. He rebounded in 1955 to win his third MVP by batting .318 with 32 homers and 107 RBI. Starting in 1956, his hand injury dating back to 1954 had caused nerve damage, and his hitting suffered further decline in 1957. He hoped for a return to form in 1958, but it never happened.

Campanella was paralyzed in a car crash during the winter between the 1957 and 1958 seasons and never played again. Confined to a wheelchair, he eventually went to work for the Los Angeles Dodgers. Inducted into the Hall of Fame in 1969, Campy said, "You got to be a man to play baseball for a living, but you got to have a lot of little boy in you, too."

MAJOR LEAGUE TOTALS

BA	G	AB	R	H	2B	3B	HR	RBI	SB
.276	1,215	4,205	627	1,161	178	18	242	856	25

ROD CAREW

SECOND BASEMAN
FIRST BASEMAN

MINNESOTA TWINS 1967-1978
CALIFORNIA ANGELS 1979-1985

◆   ◆   ◆

IN 1977, ROD CAREW MADE a valiant run at the .400 mark, but fell just short. In his career, he topped .300 15 times and .330 10 times to win seven batting titles, posting over 200 hits in four seasons.

Born in the Panama Canal Zone in 1945, Rodney Scott Carew moved to New York at age 17. He joined the Twins' organization as a second baseman in 1964 and won AL Rookie of the Year honors in 1967 by hitting .292. He took his first batting title in 1969. Minnesota won the AL West in 1969 and 1970, but Carew and Co. ran into the Baltimore buzz saw both years.

Carew won batting titles each year from 1972 to 1975. Unfortunately, the slightly built Carew took a pounding at second. Twins manager Gene Mauch moved Rod to first base to extend his career. In 1977, he responded with his run at .400, which ended with a .388 mark, a league-leading 16 triples, 239 hits, and 128 runs. It was his sixth batting title. Carew was a runaway choice as the league's Most Valuable Player.

"[Carew is] the only player in baseball who consistenly hits my grease. He sees the ball so well, I guess he can pick out the dry side."

—GAYLORD PERRY

Carew was a master bunter—in 1972, he had 15 bunt hits, but not a single home run—and astonished teammates by putting a handkerchief at various spots on the foul lines and dropping bunts onto it. In 1969, he stole home a record-tying seven times, and he swiped at least 20 sacks in seven seasons. He won his seventh and final batting title with a .333 mark in 1978.

In 1979, Carew was dealt to the California Angels and helped them reach the ALCS. In 1985, he collected his 3,000th hit and retired that fall with 3,053 safeties. In 1991, Carew was elected to the Hall of Fame in his first eligible season. That November, he was named the Angels' hitting coach. However, personal tragedy beset him, as his daughter Michelle passed away in April 1996 after a long fight with leukemia.

			MAJOR LEAGUE TOTALS						
BA	G	AB	R	H	2B	3B	HR	RBI	SB
.328	2,469	9,315	1,424	3,053	445	112	92	1,015	353

STEVE CARLTON

P I T C H E R

ST. LOUIS CARDINALS 1965-1971
PHILADELPHIA PHILLIES 1972-1986
SAN FRANCISCO GIANTS 1986
CHICAGO WHITE SOX 1986
CLEVELAND INDIANS 1987
MINNESOTA TWINS 1987-1988

◆ ◆ ◆

NEVER HAS RICE gone into such a recipe: Take one left arm and add a heap of endurance. Sprinkle with determination and independence. Throw in Eastern flavor and a vat of rice—presto, a career to savor. That's how it worked for Steve "Lefty" Carlton, who set a record with four Cy Young Awards, won 329 games, and retired in second place on the all-time strikeout list with 4,136.

Steven Norman Carlton was born in Miami in 1944. He broke into the St. Louis starting rotation in 1965 and pitched for World Series clubs in 1967 and '68. He blossomed in 1971, posting his first 20-win season. He wanted a fitting pay raise, but the Cards balked. Because of the contract dispute, Carlton was traded to Philadelphia on February 25, 1972, for Rick Wise. Within weeks, the Cardinals regretted the deal.

"When you call a pitcher 'Lefty' and everybody in both leagues knows who you mean, he must be pretty good."
—Clint Hurdle

Carlton immediately recorded a season for the ages—going 27-10 for a team that won just 59 games. He was the NL leader in wins, ERA (1.97), innings pitched (346), and strikeouts (310).

With the Phils, Carlton teamed with strength coach Gus Hoefling to intensify his training. One drill involved working his arm down through a vat of rice. Carlton also embraced some Asian philosophy.

On the mound, he focused on the catcher's glove. Steve Garvey said that Lefty's slider was almost impossible for a right-hander to hit. It broke sharply down and in, and if you got the bat on it at all, you'd probably ground it foul.

Carlton won Cy Young Awards in 1972, 1977, 1980, and 1982. He appeared in seven postseasons, going 4-2 in NLCS play and 2-2 in Series play. His best October came in 1980, when he went 1-0 in the playoffs and 2-0 in the World Series, including the clincher that gave the Phillies their first-ever world title.

Carlton's last winning season came in 1984. He retired in 1988 with five strikeout crowns and six 20-win seasons. Though the press disliked Carlton because he refused to talk to reporters, everyone respected his talent. He was elected to the Hall of Fame in 1994.

MAJOR LEAGUE TOTALS									
W	L	ERA	G	CG	IP	H	ER	BB	SO
329	244	3.22	741	254	5,217.1	4,672	1,864	1,833	4,136

GARY CARTER
CATCHER

MONTREAL EXPOS 1974-1984; 1992
NEW YORK METS 1985-1989
SAN FRANCISCO GIANTS 1990
LOS ANGELES DODGERS 1992

◆   ◆   ◆

GARY CARTER helped the Mets over the top in the mid-1980s. In order to challenge for an NL East title, they needed another big hitter and a capable catcher to guide their talented but inexperienced pitching staff. Before the 1985 season, New York shipped four players to the Montreal Expos for Carter, who promptly hit .281 with 32 home runs and led National League catchers in putouts and chances per game.

Another superb season by Carter in 1986 helped the Mets win the NL East divisional crown. The Mets finished 108-54, while Carter's 24 homers and 105 RBI led New York to a world title.

Gary Edmund Carter (born in 1954) began his major-league career in 1975 as an outfielder, batting .270 with 17 homers and 68 RBI for Montreal. By 1977, his part-time play behind the plate was so inspired that the Expos gave the starting backstopper job to Carter that June.

> *"If the Expos come up with an offer I can't refuse, I wouldn't turn it down."*
>
> —GARY CARTER

The vote of confidence inspired Carter, who hit .284 with 31 homers and 84 RBI. He proved he could be a full-time major-league catcher by pacing NL backstops in assists, putouts, and double plays. In 1979, he batted .283 with 22 more four-baggers and again led league catchers in assists, putouts, and DPs.

The Expos finished second in 1980, led by Carter's 29 homers and 101 RBI. He led National League catchers in putouts, assists, and fielding percentage. Carter hit

.293 with 29 homers and 97 RBI in 1982. In 1984, he batted .294 with 27 homers and a league-leading 106 RBI before being dealt to the Mets.

"You can count on your right hand the number of times I've hit a homer to the opposite field. About 10."

—GARY CARTER

In 1992, he returned to Montreal and closed out his great career. Carter hit 319 lifetime home runs and was a fiery and inspiring field leader. Nobody worked harder than Gary Carter.

| | | | **MAJOR LEAGUE TOTALS** | | | | | | |
BA	G	AB	R	H	2B	3B	HR	RBI	SB
.262	2,296	7,971	1,025	2,092	371	31	324	1,225	39

OSCAR CHARLESTON

OUTFIELDER
FIRST BASEMAN
MANAGER

TEAMS INCLUDE: INDIANAPOLIS ABCs, HARRISBURG GIANTS, DETROIT STARS, CHICAGO AMERICAN GIANTS, ST. LOUIS GIANTS, HOMESTEAD GRAYS, PITTSBURGH CRAWFORDS, TOLEDO CRAWFORDS, PHILADELPHIA STARS, BROOKLYN BROWN DODGERS 1915-1954

♦ ♦ ♦

OSCAR CHARLESTON put punch in the lineups of a dozen teams in his 35-year career. A barrel-chested man of great strength, he hit for power and average and ran like the wind. Only Josh Gibson challenges Oscar's reputation as a slugger, and only "Cool Papa" Bell is mentioned with him when top Negro League center fielders are named.

Born in Indianapolis, Oscar McKinley Charleston (1896-1954) began his career in 1912 in the Philippines as a member of the Army. He also ran track. Discharged in 1915, Charleston signed with the Indianapolis ABCs.

Charleston was compared to Josh Gibson as a slugger and to Cool Papa Bell as a fleet center fielder.

John B. Holway wrote: "There were three things Oscar Charleston excelled at on the field: hitting, fielding, and fighting. He loved all three, and it's a toss-up which he was best at." Each of the three is documented. Oscar's lifetime average is .357. Charleston's 11 homers against major-league pitchers in exhibition games ties for the highest recorded total. In the field, Charleston was just as impressive, with an arm more accurate than strong and the speed to run down drives in any part of the park easily.

Infielders got out of Oscar's way as he ran the bases; Charleston had considerable strength, speed, and a mean streak. Off the field he was just as formidable. Cool Papa Bell said that Charleston ripped the hood off a "mouthy" Klansman in Florida in 1935. Charleston resembled Babe Ruth in his love for women and the good life. Like the Babe, Oscar is remembered as genial and good-natured, though few were blind to his faults.

Charleston stayed on past his prime as a player-manager, mainly with the Pittsburgh Crawfords. He switched to first base after a chronic weight problem got the best of him. Charleston's legacy was finally honored by the Hall of Fame in 1976.

NEGRO LEAGUE STATS*							
BA	G	AB	H	2B	3B	HR	SB
.357	821	2,992	1,069	184	63	151	153

Note: Charleston's Negro League career stats are incomplete.

ROGER CLEMENS

PITCHER

BOSTON RED SOX 1984-1996

◆　　　◆　　　◆

ROGER CLEMENS was baseball's best pitcher during the late 1980s and early 1990s. He won three Cy Young Awards despite pitching in tiny Fenway Park.

William Roger Clemens (born in 1962) helped the University of Texas win the 1983 NCAA baseball championship. That year, the fireballer became the Red Sox's first-round draft pick.

Boston promoted Clemens in 1984, and the youngster was 9-4 despite a forearm injury. Two years later, in 1986, he helped Boston to its first World Series in a decade, compiling a 24-4 record with 10 complete games, 238 strikeouts, and a league-best 2.48 ERA. He also set a single-game big-league record by fanning 20 Seattle Mariners on April 29. Clemens was named both the AL's Cy Young winner and MVP that season.

In 1987, Roger became the first Red Sox to win 20 games back-to-back since Luis Tiant in 1973 and '74. Clemens led the AL in victories, winning percentage, complete games, and shutouts while capturing another Cy Young.

"I was pitching on all adrenaline . . . and challenging them. I was throwing the ball right down the middle of the plate."

—ROGER CLEMENS ON HIS FIRST 20-STRIKEOUT GAME

The next year, a late-season slump stopped Clemens from earning his third straight 20-win season, but he paced the AL with 291 strikeouts. In 1990, he again helped Boston to the postseason by fashioning a 21-6 mark with a 1.93 ERA. He won his third Cy Young in 1991 by pacing the AL in both ERA and strikeouts.

In 1992, he led the AL in ERA for the third consecutive time, but then he began to struggle. The next year, Clemens sat out a month with a groin pull and had a poor 11-14 record. As he began to lose some velocity off his fastball, Roger was forced to rethink his approach. Clemens worked more off-speed pitches into his repertoire in an attempt to recapture his previous level of greatness. He found his old magic on September 18, 1996, when he struck out 20 Detroit Tigers, tying his own single-game record for most Ks.

MAJOR LEAGUE TOTALS									
W	L	ERA	G	CG	IP	H	ER	BB	SO
192	111	3.07	383	100	2,776.0	2,359	948	856	2,590

ROBERTO CLEMENTE

O U T F I E L D E R

PITTSBURGH PIRATES 1955-1972

◆   ◆   ◆

ROBERTO CLEMENTE took being a role model seriously, sending out 20,000 autographed pictures a year to kids. He had one of the strongest outfield arms in history, won four batting titles, and notched 3,000 base hits. On December 31, 1972, he was on a cargo plane from Puerto Rico airlifting emergency relief supplies, bound for earthquake-torn Nicaragua. The plane crashed a mile off of the Puerto Rico coast, and there were no survivors. Clemente left behind his wife, three young sons, and millions of fans. He was elected to the Hall of Fame in an extraordinary special election held just 11 weeks after his death; he was named on 93 percent of the ballots.

Roberto Clemente y Walker (1934-1973) grew up near San Juan, Puerto Rico. He developed his strength as a youngster by unloading grocery trucks and by squeezing a rubber ball. The Pittsburgh Pirates drafted him in 1955.

"Most of what I know about style I learned from Roberto Clemente."
—JOHN SAYLES

Clemente joined the Pirates that year, and he was a good player for several years. By 1960, he began to emerge as a star, achieving personal bests in runs, home runs, RBI, and batting average. He hit .310 as the Pirates beat the Yankees in the World Series. He raised his game another notch in 1961, hitting .351, the first of five times he hit above .340.

No one who saw Clemente throw the ball could forget the power and accuracy of those throws. His arm was a deadly weapon that he could unleash from impossible angles and distances. He won

Gold Gloves every year from 1961 through 1972.

Roberto won four batting titles, hit 240 homers, and was the National League Most Valuable Player in 1966. He has perhaps the greatest defensive reputation of any right fielder in history, playing more games in right field than any player in National League history.

Although Clemente was troubled by a bad back, bone chips, and shoulder troubles throughout his career, he posted the highest batting average for the decade of the 1960s with a .328 mark. Clemente hit .312 in 1972, at age 38, and rapped his 3,000th hit on September 30. Clemente felt a duty to his fans, particularly his countrymen. He once said, "A country without idols is nothing." Clemente was an idol for many people in many countries.

MAJOR LEAGUE TOTALS									
BA	G	AB	R	H	2B	3B	HR	RBI	SB
.317	2,433	9,454	1,416	3,000	440	166	240	1,305	83

TY COBB

OUTFIELDER

DETROIT TIGERS 1906-1926
PHILADELPHIA ATHLETICS 1927-1928

◆   ◆   ◆

WHEN THE FIRST Hall of Fame vote was taken in 1936, Ty Cobb was named on 222 of the 226 ballots cast to lead all candidates for enshrinement. The shock was not that "The Georgia Peach" outpolled every other player, including Babe Ruth and Honus Wagner, but that four voters could ignore Cobb's towering credentials. This slight was understandable only when it was taken into consideration that he was not just one of the greatest players who ever lived, but he was also the most despised.

Tyrus Raymond Cobb (1886-1961) himself saw no paradox in that. Throughout his life he contended that he was far from being a great athlete. What made him such a superb player was his unparalleled desire to excel and, above all, to win. No story better illustrates both his fiery determination and the reason for his unpopularity with opponents and teammates alike than the one told about a 1905 fracas between Cobb and Nap Rucker, his roommate while both were playing in the minors for Augusta. Rucker returned to their hotel room ahead of Cobb after a game and drew a bath for himself. When Cobb found him in the tub and began upbraiding him, Rucker only looked bewildered. "Don't you understand yet?" Cobb roared. "I've got to be first all the time—in everything."

As a result of his unquenchable thirst to win and his reckless slides with spikes high whenever he tried to take a base, Cobb was shunned by other players. Some—such as Sam Crawford, who played beside Cobb in the Detroit outfield—went years without speaking to Cobb. Yet, if wanting to be first was what ignited Cobb, no one can deny that he got his wish. When he retired in 1928 after 24 seasons in the majors, he held almost every major career and single-season batting and baserunning record. Most have since been broken, but one that almost certainly never will be is his mark for the highest career batting average. Precious few players in the past half century have managed to hit .367 for one season, let alone a 24-year period.

"The great American game should be an unrelenting war of nerves."

—TY COBB

Cobb's deepest regret was that he never played on a World Series winner. The closest he came was in 1909, when the Tigers took the Pirates to seven games before losing. Only 22 at the time and playing on his third straight AL champion, Cobb seemed destined to play in more World Series before he was done. But, the 1909 classic was his last.

Whether playing for an also-run or a contender, though, Cobb gave the same relentless effort. It was thus difficult to credit a story that surfaced after he was fired as the Tigers player-manager following the 1926 season. Reportedly both he and Tris Speaker had helped rig a 1919 game between Detroit and Cleveland. The only part of the story that was consistent with the Cobb everyone knew was that it had been foreordained that Detroit would win the contest. Cobb, not even for all the money in the world, would never have agreed to finish less than first in something.

Despite the 1926 scandal, Cobb was allowed to sign with the Athletics. He retired after two seasons in Philadelphia. For the next 33 years he lived comfortably fixed but essentially alone. Cobb died in Atlanta on July 17, 1961.

MAJOR LEAGUE TOTALS									
BA	G	AB	R	H	2B	3B	HR	RBI	SB
.367	3,034	11,429	2,245	4,191	724	295	118	1,961	892

MICKEY COCHRANE

CATCHER

PHILADELPHIA ATHLETICS 1925-1933
DETROIT TIGERS 1934-1937

◆ ◆ ◆

MICKEY COCHRANE WAS, throughout his career, the best-hitting catcher in baseball. He set records for catchers with a .320 lifetime batting average and a .419 on-base average. He also had a fine batting eye, and walked four times as often as he struck out.

In 1923, Gordon Stanley Cochrane (1903-1962) signed his first minor-league contract under an assumed name, not to protect his college eligibility—he had already been a five-sport star at Boston University—but to guard his ego.

Cochrane did well, although it took him several weeks to adjust to his new position behind the plate. Soon, he caught the eye of Philadelphia A's boss Connie Mack, who took over Portland in the Pacific Coast League just to give Mickey his own place to hone his skills.

Cochrane was, throughout his career, the best-hitting catcher in baseball. He set career records for catchers with a .320 lifetime batting average and a .419 on-base average.

Joining the Mackmen in 1925, Cochrane caught a rookie-record 134 games and hit .331. In 1929, he batted .331 with 69 walks and just eight strikeouts. Mickey was far from a polished maskman, however, and some felt that he never fully mastered his trade. When Pepper Martin ran wild for the Cardinals against the A's in the 1931 World Series, Philadelphia pitcher George Earnshaw publicly blamed Cochrane.

Cochrane played on five pennant winners—three in Philadelphia and two more after he was traded to Detroit in 1933. He had early success as a player-manager, winning flags in 1934 and 1935.

Cochrane was beaned by Bumb Hadley on May 25, 1937. The pitch fractured Cochrane's skull, ending his career.

On May 25, 1937, Cochrane was beaned by New York's Bump Hadley and hovered near death for over a week before recovering. Detroit owner Walter Briggs forbade Cochrane to play again after doctors warned a second beaning could be fatal. Through as a player, Mickey managed the Tigers another one and one-half seasons. He also served in the front offices of the A's and Tigers before being named to the Hall of Fame in 1947.

MAJOR LEAGUE TOTALS									
BA	G	AB	R	H	2B	3B	HR	RBI	SB
.320	1,482	5,169	1,041	1,652	333	64	119	832	64

EDDIE COLLINS

SECOND BASEMAN

PHILADELPHIA ATHLETICS 1906-1914; 1927-1930
CHICAGO WHITE SOX 1915-1926

◆　　　◆　　　◆

JOHN McGRAW once said that Eddie Collins was the best ballplayer he'd ever seen. Connie Mack (who managed both Collins and Nap Lajoie) called Collins the best second baseman he ever saw. Those are strong endorsements coming from two men who saw a lot of baseball. Collins is arguably the greatest second baseman in history.

Edward Trowbridge Collins Sr. (1887-1951) was a college star for Columbia, but evidence that he appeared as a professional under an assumed name in six games in 1906 ended his amateur status. He joined Connie Mack's Philadelphia Athletics after graduation. Eddie teamed with

Jack Barry at shortstop, Stuffy McInnis at first, and Frank Baker at third to form the famous "$100,000 Infield." In Collins's first World Series, in 1910, he hit .429 and set four hitting records, after a regular season that included a then-record 81 stolen bases. In all, he won three championships with the A's.

Collins played 25 years in the AL as its premier offensive and defensive second baseman.

When the Athletics were broken up and sold off after the devastating salary raids of the upstart Federal League, Collins fetched the highest price paid for a player until Babe Ruth went to the Yankees. The White Sox gave $50,000 for "Cocky" after his MVP 1914 season. He led the Sox to a World Series triumph in 1917. One of the clean players on the 1919 Black Sox, Eddie never forgave the eight players who sold out. The 1919 World Series was

Eddie's last, but he left behind a stack of World Series records.

Collins hit for average and not power. He finished with a .333 lifetime batting average and a .406 career on-base average. He hit over .340 10 times and almost never struck out. Collins set many fielding records for second basemen, including most putouts, assists, and total chances. Few have been able to match Eddie's abilities and longevity. His skill at adapting his aggressive style of play to the changing style of baseball may have been his greatest asset.

Collins was named player-manager of the White Sox in 1924 but never finished higher than fifth in his two years at the helm. He returned to Philadelphia in 1927 but played less and less until he retired from playing in 1930. Eddie was enshrined in Cooperstown in 1939.

MAJOR LEAGUE TOTALS									
BA	G	AB	R	H	2B	3B	HR	RBI	SB
.333	2,826	9,949	1,818	3,311	437	187	47	1,299	743

SAM CRAWFORD

OUTFIELDER

CINCINNATI REDS 1899-1902
DETROIT TIGERS 1903-1917

◆ ◆ ◆

IN SAM CRAWFORD'S TIME, the great sluggers hit triples, not home runs. By that standard, Crawford was the dead-ball era's biggest power threat. He left the majors in 1917 with 309 triples, still the major-league record. Crawford is also the only player in this century to lead both major leagues in home runs.

Born in Wahoo, Nebraska, Samuel Earl Crawford (1880-1968) was tagged "Wahoo Sam" early in his professional career and grew so fond of the nickname that he asked that it be inscribed on his Hall of Fame plaque. He played his first pro baseball in 1899 and did so well that Cincinnati purchased him late that season.

Still just 19 years old when he debuted with the Reds, Crawford hit .307 with eight triples in 31 games.

A former barber from Nebraska, Wahoo Sam Crawford set an all-time record with 309 triples in his 19-year career, 14 more than former teammate Ty Cobb.

After the 1902 season, Crawford escaped the lowly Reds, a cellar finisher in 1901 despite his loop-leading 16 homers. Jumping to Detroit in the American League, he hit .335 in his first AL season with 25 triples. Even with Crawford's slugging, Detroit remained a second-division team until Ty Cobb came along in 1905. Playing side by side in the outfield, the pair spearheaded the 1907 to 1909 Tigers, the first team in American League history to garner three consecutive pennants. Crawford finished second to Cobb in AL batting in 1907 and '08.

Crawford fashioned a .309 career batting average and logged at least 10 triples in every full season he played. He was a loop leader in three-baggers six times and also topped the AL in RBI on three occasions.

During his 14-year tour of duty with Detroit, Crawford became very popular. This made Cobb jealous, and relations between the two deteriorated. Soon, they only spoke when calling each other off fly balls. Ironically, Ty Cobb campaigned the hardest for Crawford when he was passed over for selection to the Hall of Fame. In 1957, Crawford received the long-overdue honor.

MAJOR LEAGUE TOTALS									
BA	G	AB	R	H	2B	3B	HR	RBI	SB
.309	2,517	9,570	1,391	2,961	458	309	97	1,525	366

JOE CRONIN

SHORTSTOP

PITTSBURGH PIRATES 1926-1927
WASHINGTON SENATORS 1928-1934
BOSTON RED SOX 1935-1945

MANAGER

WASHINGTON SENATORS 1933-1934
BOSTON RED SOX 1935-1947
1,236-1,055

◆   ◆   ◆

A T AGE 20 IN 1926, Joe Cronin sat on the bench, was farmed out, and then sold. In 1959, he became president of the American League. Between, he turned in a Hall of Fame career as a great offensive shortstop.

Joseph Edward Cronin (1906-1984) was born in San Francisco a few months after the great earthquake. Cronin played semipro ball after graduation. A Pittsburgh scout signed Joe in 1925, and after a good season with Johnstown in the Mid-

Atlantic League, Cronin was promoted to the Pirates. He then sat behind Glenn Wright for two seasons.

Cronin moved to the AL, landing in Washington in 1928. He had a decent campaign in 1929, and followed it up with a *Sporting News* MVP season in 1930. He hit .346 with 127 runs scored and 126 RBI. Cronin totaled 100 RBI eight times. He compiled a lifetime .301 batting average, hitting over .300 in 11 seasons. He socked 51 doubles in 1938 and hit 515 in his career. He was named outstanding major-league shortstop by *The Sporting News* seven times.

Active in an era when player-managers were common, Cronin served a long term in that role. He ran the Senators in 1933 and 1934, and he skippered the Red Sox from 1935 to '47 after Boston purchased him. His debut season as manager produced a pennant in 1933, and he hit .318 in that fall's World Series. Ted Williams said in 1946 that Cronin was "the greatest manager I ever played for." Cronin finished first again in 1946, the year he retired as a player, and brought Boston its first pennant since 1918.

When Cronin finished second in 1933 in the voting for the AL MVP Award, it was the highest finish ever by a Washington player in MVP balloting.

In 1959, Joe was the first former player to be elected AL president. During his tenure, he oversaw the league's growth from eight to 12 teams and was instrumental in formulating divisional play. He remained in office until 1973.

MAJOR LEAGUE TOTALS									
BA	G	AB	R	H	2B	3B	HR	RBI	SB
.301	2,124	7,579	1,233	2,285	515	118	170	1,424	87

DIZZY DEAN
PITCHER

St. Louis Cardinals 1930; 1932-1937
Chicago Cubs 1938-1941
St. Louis Browns 1947

◆   ◆   ◆

ONE OF THE MOST entertaining players ever, Dizzy Dean blazed bright in baseball's sky for five seasons. He was the last NL pitcher to win 30 games in a season, was the league's Most Valuable Player in 1934, and finished second in the voting in 1935 and 1936.

"The good lord was kind to me. He gave me a strong body, a good right arm, and a weak mind."

—DIZZY DEAN

Jay Hanna Dean (1911-1974) honed his pitching skills—and got his nickname—in the Army, and a Cardinals scout signed him in 1930. Dean was 25-10 that year in the minors and tossed a three-hit shutout for the Cardinals on the final day of the season. He was summoned by St. Louis in 1932 and won 18 games, led the NL in shutouts and innings pitched, and won his first of four straight strikeout titles for the fun-loving "Gashouse Gang."

Dizzy was a natural clown but also a shrewd negotiator. He staged a holdout during the 1934 season for his brother, and fellow Redbirds pitcher, Paul, who Diz felt was underpaid. Despite missing some starts, the elder Dean went 30-7, and Paul was 19-11.

"A lot of folks that ain't saying 'ain't' ain't eating."

— DIZZY DEAN

The Deans won all of the Cardinals' World Series triumphs that year against the Detroit Tigers. While pinch-running in Game 4, Dizzy was hit in the forehead by a throw. Some feared a serious injury, but the next day's headlines read, "X-Ray of Dean's Head Reveals Nothing." Dizzy pitched a shutout in the deciding seventh game.

During the 1937 All-Star Game, a line drive broke Dizzy's toe. He came back too soon, and in doing so altered his motion, which injured his right arm. He never fully recovered, and retired in 1941 at age 30 with 150 career victories. Hall of Fame honors followed in 1953. He became a popular broadcaster infamous for malapropisms. Responding that he was ruining students' syntax, Diz said, "Sin tax? What will those fellers in Washington think of next?"

MAJOR LEAGUE TOTALS									
W	L	ERA	G	CG	IP	H	ER	BB	SO
150	83	3.02	317	154	1,967.1	1,925	660	453	1,163

MARTIN DIHIGO

OUTFIELDER
PITCHER
INFIELDER
CATCHER
MANAGER

TEAMS INCLUDE: CUBAN STARS, HOMESTEAD GRAYS, PHILADELPHIA HILLDALES, BALTIMORE BLACK SOX, NEW YORK CUBANS 1923-1945

◆　　　◆　　　◆

SINCE NEGRO LEAGUE TEAMS obtained slender profit margins, squads often consisted of 14 to 18 players. The most valuable player was usually the one who played several positions. Martin Dihigo could pitch and play seven positions (all but catcher) at an All-Star level.

Born in Matanzas, Cuba, Martin Dihigo (1905-1971) began his pro career in 1923 in the Cuban Winter League as a 17-year-old strong-armed, weak-hitting outfielder. Legend has it that his arm was so strong that he won a distance-throwing contest against a jai alai player who was allowed to use his wicker-basket cesta.

Like many Negro Leaguers, Martin played all over North, Central, and South America. Unlike most, he starred almost everywhere he saw action.

"[Dihigo] was the only guy I ever saw who could play all nine positions, run, and was a switch-hitter. I thought I was havin' a pretty good year myself down there, and they were walkin' him to get to me."

—JOHNNY MIZE

From the time he came to America (in 1923) through 1936, he made only occasional forays to the pitching mound, but Dihigo pitched more often when he played in Latin America. His pitching stats include an 18-2 record and an 0.90 ERA in 1938. He twirled the first no-hitter in Mexican League history. According to the latest available records, he won 256 games while dropping only 136.

Dihigo developed into a top hitter. He hit over .400 three times. He paced his league in homers in 1926 and in 1935. He posted a .316 career average in the Negro Leagues between 1923 and 1945.

In the field, he tossed out runners at home plate with frightening regularity. Dihigo often pitched in relief, especially as a manager. He threw no-hitters in Venezuela, Puerto Rico, and Mexico, and skippered professional clubs in America, Mexico, and Cuba until 1950.

After his retirement, Dihigo became a broadcaster and Cuba's Minister of Sport. He is the only player in the Cuban, Mexican, and American Halls of Fame.

NEGRO LEAGUE STATS*

BA	G	AB	H	2B	3B	HR	SB
.316	415	1,435	453	53	18	64	32
W	L	G	CG	IP	H	BB	SO
27	21	50	32	309	235	61	126

*Note: Dihigo's Negro League career stats are incomplete.

JOE DiMAGGIO

O U T F I E L D E R

NEW YORK YANKEES 1936-1942; 1946-1951

◆   ◆   ◆

IF JOE DIMAGGIO wasn't the greatest all-around player in baseball history, he almost certainly was the most majestic.

Joseph Paul DiMaggio (born in 1914) was a native of San Francisco, where he and his brothers Vince and Dom played baseball on the sandlots hour after hour. Joe left high school early to work in a cannery and to play semipro baseball. At age 17, he signed with the San Francisco Seals at the end of the 1932 season. Joe played in three games and batted .222. The next season, he had a .340 batting average, 28 homers, and 169 RBI in 187 games. Joe was a local hero.

DiMaggio batted .341 in 1934, but he suffered a knee injury that scared some big-league clubs away, especially at the price that the Seals were demanding. The Yankees had no such qualms; with their superior financial position, the Bombers were able to risk the $25,000 and five minor-leaguers for Joe.

DiMaggio lived up to even tough New York standards, joining with Lou Gehrig to power the Yankees to the first of four consecutive world championships in his 1936 rookie season. Although he was severely hampered by Yankee Stadium's cavernous left field, DiMaggio twice led the AL in home runs and twice in slugging. He hit only 148 of his 361 lifetime home runs at home.

DiMaggio was an outstanding and beautiful defensive outfielder. The Yankee Clipper played center with grace and threw the ball with terrific power. He led the league in assists with 22 his rookie year, and had 21 and then 20 before the league apparently got wise and stopped running on him.

Joltin' Joe won his first Most Valuable Player Award in 1939, when he had his career-best .381 batting average. When he won his second MVP in 1941, he had 76 walks and only 13 strikeouts. He also hit in a record 56 consecutive games, a feat considered the greatest in baseball history by some observers. No other hitter has ever hit in more than 44. He almost never struck out—his high was 39, his rookie year—and actually came close to having more lifetime homers than Ks, with 369 strikeouts to his 361 round-trippers.

"There may be some kid who is seeing me for the first or last time. I owe him my best."

—JOE DiMAGGIO

If Yankee Stadium depressed his career totals, World War II was even more of a factor as DiMaggio lost three seasons. He won his third MVP and the Yankees won another championship in 1947 (it was Joe that hit the drive that made Al Gionfriddo famous), but a heel injury slowed Joe in 1948, and he couldn't return to the lineup until June of 1949. His return was memorable, as he was 5-for-11 with four homers and nine RBI in a double-header. Another world championship followed, the first of five straight for the Yanks, but DiMaggio would only stick around for three of them. Injuries and the grind of the road drove him into retirement after the 1951 season. He was succeeded in center by Mickey Mantle.

With time, DiMaggio's legend continued to grow to an enormous magnitude. Ernest Hemingway used Joe as a symbol in *The Old Man and the Sea*. Musicians from Les Brown to Paul Simon wrote about DiMaggio in songs. Marilyn Monroe married Joe. DiMaggio was inducted into the Hall of Fame in 1955.

MAJOR LEAGUE TOTALS									
BA	G	AB	R	H	2B	3B	HR	RBI	SB
.325	1,736	6,821	1,390	2,214	389	131	361	1,537	30

BUCK EWING

CATCHER
INFIELDER
OUTFIELDER

TROY TROJANS 1880-1882
NEW YORK GIANTS 1883-1889; 1891-1892
NEW YORK GIANTS (PL) 1890
CLEVELAND SPIDERS 1893-1894
CINCINNATI REDS 1895-1897

◆   ◆   ◆

WILLIAM BUCKINGHAM EWING'S statistics seem noteworthy but hardly extraordinary. He led the National League in home runs in 1883 and in triples in 1884, but his career accomplishments appear modest. In Ewing's case, however, statistics deceive. In 1919, famed sportswriter Francis Richter deemed Ewing, Ty Cobb, and Honus Wagner the three greatest players in baseball history, stating that Ewing might have been the best of all.

Ewing (1859-1906) was not a very strong batsman at the beginning of his career, hitting just .250 with Troy in 1881, his first full big-league season. Eventually, he became a speedy and sometimes powerful leadoff hitter. He notched a .303 lifetime batting average, with 1,129 runs scored in 1,315 games and 336 stolen bases. From the outset of his 18-year career, Buck was viewed as a peerless defensive catcher and field leader.

"It wastes time to straigten up."
—BUCK EWING, ON WHY HE WAS THE FIRST CATCHER TO THROW TO SECOND FROM THE CROUCH

Ewing was one of the first to catalogue opposing batters' weaknesses during pregame clubhouse meetings, and he was among the first catchers to throw from a crouch. John Foster wrote that "as a thrower to bases, Ewing never had a superior . . . it was said, 'he handed the ball to the second baseman from the batter's box.'"

Catchers in the 1800s seldom worked more than half of their team's games. While most backstops simply took frequent days off, Ewing was good enough to fill in anywhere on the diamond. In 1889, with the Giants fighting for the pennant, Ewing even pitched two complete-game victories. He jumped to the Players' League the following year and was named player-manager of the New York Giants.

Ewing finished his playing career for Cincinnati in 1897. He succumbed to diabetes on October 20, 1906. In 1936, Buck tied for first place in the initial vote of the old-timers for the Hall of Fame.

					MAJOR LEAGUE TOTALS				
BA	G	AB	R	H	2B	3B	HR	RBI	SB
.303	1,315	5,363	1,129	1,625	250	178	70	738	336

Bob Feller

Pitcher

Cleveland Indians 1936-1941; 1945-1956

◆　　　◆　　　◆

B OB FELLER was probably harmed more than any other great player by World War II. Had Feller's career proceeded without interruption, instead of losing nearly four full seasons, he might be considered the greatest pitcher in history.

Born in 1918 in Iowa, Robert William Andrew Feller was signed by Cleveland in 1935 while still in high school. The signing was illegal according to the rules of the time, but Commissioner Kenesaw Mountain Landis feared a bidding war among the other teams if Feller was made a free agent, and let the deal stand.

Feller debuted with Cleveland in a July 1936 exhibition game against the Cardinals. Though only 17, Feller fanned eight Redbirds in the three innings he hurled.

Plate umpire Bob Ormsby labeled Feller the fastest pitcher he had ever seen.

However, batters learned that while Feller was unhittable, they could simply wait for walks. In 1938, he topped the majors with 240 strikeouts and set a modern single-game record with 18 Ks. However, he also allowed 208 walks.

"When I pick up the ball and it feels nice and light and small, I know I'm going to have a good day. But if I pick it up and it's big and heavy, I know I'm liable to get into a little trouble."
— BOB FELLER

His control improving, Feller paced the American League in wins during each of the next three seasons before entering the Navy. In 1940, Feller tossed the first Opening Day no-hitter in AL history and helped the Tribe finish second that year.

Returning from the war, Feller had his finest season in 1946 with 26 wins and

348 strikeouts. An arm injury in 1947 curtailed his fastball thereafter, but he continued to be one of the game's top hurlers until 1955.

"Every day is a new opportunity. You can build on yesterday's success or put its failures behind and start over again."

—Bob Feller

The author of three career no-hitters and 12 one-hit games, Feller finished his career with a 266-162 record and a 3.25 earned run average with 2,581 strikeouts in 3,827 innings pitched. He was elected to the Hall of Fame in 1962.

			MAJOR LEAGUE TOTALS						
W	L	ERA	G	CG	IP	H	ER	BB	SO
266	162	3.25	570	279	3,827	3,271	1,384	1,764	2,581

ROLLIE FINGERS

PITCHER

OAKLAND ATHLETICS 1968-1976
SAN DIEGO PADRES 1977-1980
MILWAUKEE BREWERS 1981-1985

◆   ◆   ◆

AFTER PROMOTING Rollie Fingers from the minors in 1969, the Athletics shuttled him between starting and the bullpen. Finally in 1971, Oakland manager Dick Williams decided Fingers was best suited for relief work. Rollie responded with 17 saves that year and 21 in 1972. As baseball's first superstar career reliever, Fingers redefined the closer's role.

Clean shaven when he reached the majors, Roland Glen Fingers (born in 1946) soon grew the longest mustache, tip to tip, in major-league history. His career high-point came in the 1974 World Series against the Dodgers. With the A's shooting for their third world championship in a row, Fingers won the first game of the Series and then saved the final two contests. For his efforts, Fingers earned Series MVP honors.

In June 1976, A's owner Charlie Finley tried to sell Fingers and Joe Rudi to the Red Sox, but Commissioner Bowie Kuhn voided the sale, citing the "best interests of baseball."

After two more seasons, Fingers became a free agent and signed a five-year deal with the Padres. In each of his first two seasons in San Diego, he topped the NL in saves. In 1980, Rollie was swapped to the Cardinals and then immediately shipped to Milwaukee in the year's biggest deal.

Fingers's finest season was the strike-abbreviated 1981 campaign. In 47 appearances, he collected a major-league-leading 28 saves and etched a 1.04 ERA. His banner year garnered him the MVP and Cy Young Awards. When the Brewers won their first pennant in 1982, an ailing elbow kept Fingers out of their World Series loss to the Cardinals.

In 1981, Fingers figured in more than 50 percent of the Milwaukee Brewers' victories.

Elbow problems shelved Fingers for all of 1983, but he posted 23 saves and a 1.96 ERA in 1984. The 1985 campaign proved to be his last, however, when a back injury led to a 1 6 record. Fingers and his 341 career saves (a major-league record when he retired) were voted to the Hall of Fame in 1992.

W	L	ERA	G	SV	IP	H	ER	BB	SO
114	118	2.90	944	341	1,701.0	1,474	548	492	1,299

MAJOR LEAGUE TOTALS

CARLTON FISK

C A T C H E R

Boston Red Sox 1969-1980
Chicago White Sox 1981-1993

◆　　　　◆　　　　◆

CARLTON FISK retired with major-league records for games caught and home runs by a catcher, but he is best remembered for his game-winning home run for the Boston Red Sox in the sixth game of the 1975 World Series—a world championship series many consider the best of all time.

In that game, the Reds and the Red Sox were tied in the bottom of the 12th inning when Fisk stepped to the plate. The image of Fisk swinging, watching the ball sail, and waving his arms to encourage it to stay fair is truly memorable.

Carlton Ernest Fisk (born in 1947) was drafted by the Red Sox in 1967 and began his professional career the next year. Fisk

cracked the Red Sox lineup in 1972, leading the AL with nine triples. His play
earned him American League Rookie of
the Year honors.

In 1973, "Pudge" slammed 26 homers,
but he missed most of 1974 and some of
1975 with injuries. Following a subpar
1976 season, Carlton rebounded in 1977
to hit .315 with 26 homers and 103 runs
batted in.

*On August 17, 1990, Fisk hit his
329th homer as a catcher, breaking
Johnny Bench's career record.*

After the 1980 season, Fisk became a
free agent and signed with the White Sox.
Chicago was desperate both for offense
and for an on-field general with major-
league experience. Fisk helped the Sox to
a 1983 division title, hitting .289 with 26
homers and 86 RBI. Plagued by injuries in
1984, he still had 21 homers. The next season, he returned with career highs in

homers (37) and RBI (107). He credited his comeback to an extensive training program, which he maintained the rest of his career.

"Pudge is so old, they didn't have history class when he went to school."
—STEVE LYONS

In 1990, Fisk smashed Johnny Bench's mark of most homers by a catcher; in 1993, Carlton broke Bob Boone's record for most games caught. Shortly afterward, the White Sox released him, and Fisk retired with 376 career round-trippers and a .269 average.

MAJOR LEAGUE TOTALS									
BA	G	AB	R	H	2B	3B	HR	RBI	SB
.269	2,499	8,756	1,276	2,356	421	47	376	1,330	128

WHITEY FORD

NEW YORK YANKEES 1950; 1953-1967

◆   ◆   ◆

WHITEY FORD was the ace of the 1950s New York Yankees' pitching staff. His .690 career winning percentage is the best of any modern 200-game winner. Ford's teams won 11 pennants and seven World Series, helped largely by Whitey's streak of 33 scoreless Series innings.

"There's no easier pitch to hit than a spitter that doesn't do anything."

—WHITEY FORD

Edward Charles Ford (born in 1926) of New York City started pitching only as a senior in high school. He started his pro career in 1947 with a 13-4 record and led the Eastern League with a 1.61 ERA in 1949.

Summoned to New York in mid-1950, Ford went 9-1 in 12 starts and tossed a shutout in that fall's World Series. He served two years in the military, then returned in 1953 with an 18-6 mark to help the Yankees win their fifth straight world championship.

In 1967, Ford retired with a .690 career winning percentage, the best in baseball history among 200-game winners.

Whitey didn't just win, he won often. In 12 seasons, he was at least six games over .500 each year. He led the AL with 18 wins in 1955 and a 2.47 ERA in 1956. Yankee manager Casey Stengel usually used Ford only against good teams and refused to overwork his star.

When Ralph Houk took the Yankee reins in 1961, he unleashed Whitey, who responded with a 25-4 record in a league-high 39 starts to win the Cy Young Award.

In 1963, he was 24-7, leading the AL in starts and innings pitched.

Ford used several pitches, most of them legal. The threat of his spitball kept hitters guessing, and may have helped him more than the actual pitch itself.

Whitey (dubbed the "Chairman of the Board"), his buddy Mickey Mantle, and other Yankees loved the night life. And they became a fixture on the New York club scene during the 1950s and early 1960s. Ford and Mantle each joined the Hall of Fame in 1974.

				MAJOR LEAGUE TOTALS					
W	L	ERA	G	CG	IP	H	ER	BB	SO
236	106	2.75	498	156	3,170.1	2,788	967	1,086	1,956

JIMMIE FOXX

FIRST BASEMAN

PHILADELPHIA ATHLETICS 1925-1935
BOSTON RED SOX 1936-1942
CHICAGO CUBS 1942; 1944
PHILADELPHIA PHILLIES 1945

◆   ◆   ◆

IN AN ERA OF BIG HITTERS, Jimmie Foxx won four home run titles and two batting titles. He was the first American Leaguer to be named the Most Valuable Player in consecutive seasons and the first man to win the MVP Award three times.

James Emory Foxx (1907-1967) grew up on a farm in rural Maryland. He enjoyed both high school track and baseball, and through his athletic ability and immense home runs he became celebrated. Foxx made his major-league debut as a 17-year-old with the Philadelphia A's in 1925. From 1926 to 1928, he was a utility player, backing up Mickey Cochrane at catcher and playing first and third.

By the time Foxx became the regular first baseman in 1929, the A's were a powerhouse. "Double X" formed with Al Simmons and Lefty Grove the heart of Connie Mack's last great team, and the Athletics appeared in three consecutive World Series from 1929 to 1931. Jimmie won consecutive MVP Awards in 1932 and '33. He had 169 RBI and 58 homers in 1932, and he earned the Triple Crown in 1933 with 48 homers, 163 RBI, and a .356 average. The A's won two championships before bowing to St. Louis in seven games in 1931. That was to be Foxx's postseason swan song. He hit .344 and slugged .609 in 18 World Series games.

"Jimmie Foxx wasn't scouted; he was trapped."

—LEFTY GOMEZ

Because Mack suffered economically during the Depression, he sold Foxx to Boston in 1936. Ted Williams said: "Jimmie Foxx with all those muscles, hitting drives that sounded like gunfire. Crraack. A hell of a lot louder than mine sounded." Jimmie hailed his arrival by hitting 41 homers with 143 RBI in '36.

Though Foxx's career began to be affected by his age and lifestyle, he had enough left for a final burst. After "slumping" to 36 homers, 127 RBI, and a career-low .285 average in 1937, he bounced back in 1938. Foxx hit 50 homers and led the league in RBI and average, winning his third MVP Award. Appendicitis shortened his terrific 1939 season, and 1940 was his last decent year.

When he retired in 1945, only Babe Ruth had more home runs, and Jimmie slammed more homers than anyone in the decade of the 1930s. He had three seasons with slugging averages of over .700. Foxx was inducted into the Hall of Fame in 1951.

				MAJOR LEAGUE TOTALS						
BA	G	AB	R	H	2B	3B	HR	RBI	SB
.325	2,317	8,134	1,751	2,646	458	125	534	1,921	88

LOU GEHRIG

FIRST BASEMAN

NEW YORK YANKEES 1923-1939

◆   ◆   ◆

ON JUNE 2, 1925, when New York Yankees backup first sacker Fred Merkle, who was giving the club's long-time regular Wally Pipp a day off, seemed about to collapse from the heat, manager Miller Huggins called on rookie first baseman Lou Gehrig as a late-inning replacement. From that point on, Gehrig played a record 2,130 consecutive games for the Yankees. Only very rarely did he play for the sole reason of extending his monumental streak. He played because he was the best all-around first baseman in baseball history.

Born in Manhattan, Henry Louis Gehrig (1903-1941) starred in all sports at the High School of Commerce. After two years at Columbia University, Gehrig accepted a bonus of $1,500 from the Yankees against his father's wishes and began playing with Hartford of the Eastern League. A two-year apprenticeship in the minors was all he needed before he was ready to take his place among the game's greats.

In his first full season (1925), Gehrig hit .295, scored 73 runs, and knocked home 68 teammates. He would never again tally under 100 runs or collect less than 100 RBI in a full season. Lou averaged the highest number of runs and RBI per game of any 20th century player.

"[Gehrig] was a symbol of indestructibility—a Gibraltar in cleats."

—JIM MURRAY

In 1931, Gehrig established an American League record when he netted 184 RBI, breaking his own old mark of 175 set in 1927. The following year, he became the first player in the 20th century to clout four home runs in a game. He also once had three triples in a game that was rained out in the fourth inning. When Lou left baseball he had 493 home runs, second at the time only to Babe Ruth.

Gehrig's slugging exploits were only part of the story. He was also both an excellent baserunner and a solid first baseman. He was extremely consistent and, of course, durable. Twice he was selected the AL's MVP, and he was always known for his overall performance.

In 1934, Gehrig won the Triple Crown while copping his only batting title with a .363 mark. Two years later he garnered his final home run crown with 49 four-baggers, tying his own personal high. When Gehrig's batting average slipped to .295 in 1938 and his RBI and homer totals also dipped, it seemed just an off year at first. The strange slump persisted into the next season, restricting him to a meager four singles in his first eight games. When teammates began congratulating him for making routine plays, Lou knew the time had come to step down. On May 2, 1939, he took himself out of the lineup for the first time in nearly 14 years. A few weeks later he entered the Mayo Clinic for tests, which revealed that he had amyotrophic lateral sclerosis—a hardening of the spinal cord. The rare disease has no known cure and is always terminal. Knowing he would soon die, Gehrig retired formally on July 4, 1939, in a special ceremony at Yankee Stadium. Tearfully, he told the packed house, "Today, I consider myself the luckiest man on the face of the Earth."

Following the 1939 season, Gehrig took a job with the New York City Parole Commission. He continued to work with youth groups and to play bridge with his wife, Eleanor, and close friends until just a few weeks before his death on June 2, 1941. That same year he was inducted into the Hall of Fame.

MAJOR LEAGUE TOTALS									
BA	G	AB	R	H	2B	3B	HR	RBI	SB
.340	2,164	8,001	1,888	2,721	535	162	493	1,990	102

CHARLIE GEHRINGER

DETROIT TIGERS 1924-1942

◆   ◆   ◆

NEVER FLAMBOYANT, the almost Sphinx-like Charlie Gehringer might have gone virtually unnoticed on the baseball diamond but for his outstanding day-in, day-out performance. His unceasing excellence led to his nickname, "The Mechanical Man." Gehringer's manager Mickey Cochrane said of him, "He says hello on opening day and goodbye on closing day, and in between he hits .350."

Charles Leonard Gehringer (1903-1993) played both football and baseball at the University of Michigan and was given a tryout by none other than Detroit player-manager Ty Cobb. Signed by the Tigers in 1924 as a third baseman, Gehringer soon moved to second and became the club's regular second-sacker in 1926, where he remained for 16 years. After hitting .277 as a rookie, he batted over .300 nearly every season until 1941. As a defensive player, Gehringer had few peers. He led the AL in fielding percentage six times and paced the loop in assists seven times.

"I had most of my trouble with left-handed hitters. Charlie Gehringer could hit me in a tunnel at midnight with the lights out."

—LEFTY GOMEZ

Gehringer's high-water mark came in 1937 when he rapped .371 to win the American League batting crown. Before that year, Gehringer also paced the junior loop on several occasions in runs, hits, doubles, triples, and stolen bases. His play in all departments was of such high caliber that he played in six All-Star Games, hitting .500. He displayed the same steady brilliance in three World Series appearances with the Tigers. In 81 fall classic at bats, Charlie hit .321, one point higher than his career average of .320.

"Us ballplayers do things backwards. First we play, then we retire and go to work."

—CHARLIE GEHRINGER

Gehringer retired at the end of the 1942 season with 2,839 hits and a .320 average and ended his career by leading the AL in pinch hits. Two years after he was elected to the Hall of Fame in 1949, Charlie returned to the Tigers as general manager. He subsequently served as a Tiger vice president until 1959.

MAJOR LEAGUE TOTALS									
BA	G	AB	R	H	2B	3B	HR	RBI	SB
.320	2,323	8,860	1,774	2,839	574	146	184	1,427	182

BOB GIBSON

PITCHER

ST. LOUIS CARDINALS 1959-1975

◆　　　◆　　　◆

IN THE 1960s, when power pitchers ruled the game, few were as dominant as Bob Gibson. Among the most successful of World Series performers, he set many records during his 17-year Hall of Fame career with the St. Louis Cardinals.

"Bob Gibson is the luckiest pitcher I ever saw. He always pitches when the other team doesn't score any runs."

—TIM MCCARVER

Robert Gibson (born in 1935) overcame both the slums of Omaha, Nebraska, and childhood illness to become an outstanding athlete. The Cardinals signed him in 1957, and he soon made it to the major leagues. However, poor control kept him from success until 1961, when Cardinals manager Johnny Keane put Gibson in the starting rotation.

Gibson led the league in walks that year, but won 13 games. The following season he had 208 strikeouts, the first of nine seasons of 200-plus Ks. In 1963, he was 18-9, and in 1964, his 19-12 record led the Cardinals to a world title. Gibson was intimidating in Series play, winning an NL-record seven games against two losses as the Cards took world championships in 1964 and 1967, and lost in 1968.

"I guess I was never much in awe of anybody. I think you have to have that attitude if you're going to go far in this game."

—BOB GIBSON

In 1968, Gibson won both the MVP and Cy Young Awards. His record was 22-9, with an NL-record 1.12 ERA and a league-best 268 strikeouts. In Game 1 of the World Series that year, he had a single-game-record 17 strikeouts.

Pride played a huge role in Gibson's character and his success. As with other African-American players, he was forced to stay in a private home during his first spring training, in 1958, and the struggle to overcome racism stayed with him. He helped force the Cardinals' Florida hotels to accept blacks in the early 1960s.

Gibson won another Cy Young in 1970 with a 23-7 showing. He had more than 20 wins in five seasons and won in double figures 14 consecutive years. Gibson also smacked 24 lifetime home runs and won nine consecutive Gold Gloves.

MAJOR LEAGUE TOTALS									
W	L	ERA	G	CG	IP	H	ER	BB	SO
251	174	2.91	528	255	3,884.2	3,279	1,258	1,336	3,117

JOSH GIBSON

C A T C H E R

TEAMS INCLUDE: HOMESTEAD GRAYS, PITTSBURGH CRAWFORDS, 1930-1946

◆　　　　◆　　　　◆

POSSIBLY the best known of the Negro League sluggers, Josh Gibson's tape-measure home runs rattled off the seats at a rate that could not be ignored.

Joshua Gibson (1911-1947) was born in Buena Vista, Georgia. Josh's father, wishing to give his children a better chance in life, moved the family to Pittsburgh, where Josh grew up. An outstanding athlete, Josh won medals as a swimmer before turning full attention to baseball. Working at an air-brake factory at age 16, he was a star for an all-black amateur team.

Gibson was playing semipro ball by 1929. He was watching a Homestead

Grays game when their catcher split a finger. They pulled Josh out of the stands and put a Grays uniform on him. Within two years he was one of the team's biggest stars. Though he was barely in his 20s, Gibson was hitting around 70 home runs a year. He was lured to the Pittsburgh Crawfords in 1932, where he caught Satchel Paige for five years.

> *"Josh Gibson was, at the minimum, two Yogi Berras."*
>
> —BILL VEECK

Gibson was a catcher from the beginning, but he was not polished at the beginning. Since he played more than 200 games a year, with summer in the States and winter in either Mexico or the Dominican Republic, Josh became a veteran backstop in little time. Roy Campanella called Gibson "not only the greatest catcher but the greatest ballplayer I ever saw."

Gibson reached distances in major-league parks undreamed of by the white players who played in them regularly. He is credited with hitting a ball out of Yankee Stadium, and his longest hits are variously estimated between 575 and 700 feet. His career total is uncertain, but even the lowest estimates put him ahead of Hank Aaron, with 800 to 950 career homers. Gibson's lifetime average is the highest in Negro baseball, at .354 and higher, depending on your source.

Gibson went back to the Grays in 1936, but began to suffer from headaches. He drank more than was his habit, partly in a search for relief from what was finally diagnosed a brain tumor. He died in 1947, at age 36, one day after Jackie Robinson played his first game for Montreal in the Dodger farm system.

NEGRO LEAGUE STATS*							
BA	G	AB	H	2B	3B	HR	SB
.354	439	1,820	644	110	45	141	17

*Note: Gibson's Negro League stats are incomplete.

GOOSE GOSLIN

OUTFIELDER

WASHINGTON SENATORS 1921-1930; 1933; 1937
ST. LOUIS BROWNS 1930-1932
DETROIT TIGERS 1933-1936

◆　　　◆　　　◆

NICKNAMED "GOOSE" because of his last name and because of his large nose, Leon Allen Goslin (1900-1971) was originally a pitcher, but he moved to the outfield when his first professional manager thought that Goose's bat had more promise than his arm.

While Goslin was leading the Sally League in hitting, Washington bought him for $6,000. Unfortunately, Goslin injured his arm while heaving a shotput early in 1922 and never again threw with his same ability. Mediocre defensively even before the injury, Goslin worked hard to become a competent outfielder.

Goose quickly emerged, though, as a standout slugger. In 1923 and 1925, he led the American League in triples. A year later he was the loop's RBI king. Even though he was a fine power hitter, Goslin could not rack up high home run totals while playing in Washington. The outfield fences in Griffith Stadium, his home park, were so distant that no Senator won a home run crown until the park was reconfigured in the 1950s. All 17 of Goslin's home runs in 1926 were hit on the road.

"I loved to play against the Yankees, especially in Yankee Stadium. Boy, did I get a kick out of beating those guys. They were so great, you know, it was a thrill to beat them."

—GOOSE GOSLIN

The Senators took AL pennants in 1924 and 1925 with Goslin's help. He won the 1928 AL batting crown, hitting .379, but in 1930 was dealt to the Browns.

Washington owner Clark Griffith almost immediately regretted letting Goose go and worked to get him back. Reobtained in December 1932, Goslin helped the Senators win their third and last pennant the following summer. Griffith then swapped Goslin to Detroit.

In 1924, Goslin was the first Washington Senator to lead the American League in runs batted in. He had 129 RBI that season.

Goslin helped the Tigers win AL titles in 1934 and 1935, and he produced the hit that won the 1935 World Series. Owner of a .316 lifetime average, 2,735 base hits, and 1,609 RBI, Goose entered the Hall of Fame in 1968.

MAJOR LEAGUE TOTALS									
BA	G	AB	R	H	2B	3B	HR	RBI	SB
.316	2,287	8,655	1,483	2,735	500	173	248	1,609	175

HARMON KILLEBREW

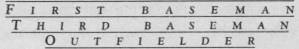

FIRST BASEMAN
THIRD BASEMAN
OUTFIELDER

WASHINGTON SENATORS 1954-1960
MINNESOTA TWINS 1961-1974
KANSAS CITY ROYALS 1975

THE TOP right-handed home run hitter in AL history, Harmon Killebrew had more than 40 home runs eight times and more than 100 RBI in 10 seasons. He won six AL homer crowns and slugged 573 career homers in 22 years.

Born in 1936, Harmon Clayton Killebrew was an all-state high school quarterback in Idaho. At 17, he was recommended to the Senators by Idaho Senator Herman Walker, who wanted to see his young constituent in the major leagues. Killebrew blasted a 435-foot homer for scout Ossie Bluege, who signed "Killer" immediately.

Harmon was a third baseman when he came up, and though he eventually played more games at first than third, he had significant playing time at the hot corner until 1971. He eventually earned outstanding AL left fielder, third baseman, and first baseman honors from *The Sporting News.*

> *"[Killebrew] has enough power to hit home runs in any park—including Yellowstone."*
>
> —PAUL RICHARDS

Killebrew, a bonus baby, didn't play full-time until 1959. He was ready for the role, leading the league with 42 home runs. He hit 31 the next year, after which the Senators became the Minnesota Twins. Harmon hit 46 for his adoring new fans in 1961, but that year Roger Maris hit 15 more. Killebrew led the league in 1962, 1963, and 1964, hitting 142 long balls in the three seasons and driving in 333 runs.

Killebrew won the AL MVP Award in 1969 with 49 homers, 140 RBI, and 145 walks, leading the league with a .430 on-base percentage. He paced the league four times in walks. Though criticized for low batting averages, his on-base totals were among the best in the league.

Killebrew's career-high batting average as a regular came in 1961, an expansion year, when he hit .288.

Harmon's 90 homers in 1969 and 1970 helped the Twins win two AL West division titles. Age and knee problems slowed Harmon in the 1970s, and he retired after the 1975 season. He was inducted into the Hall of Fame in 1984.

MAJOR LEAGUE TOTALS									
BA	G	AB	R	H	2B	3B	HR	RBI	SB
.256	2,435	8,147	1,283	2,086	290	24	573	1,584	19

SANDY KOUFAX

P I T C H E R

BROOKLYN DODGERS 1955-1957
LOS ANGELES DODGERS 1958-1966

◆   ◆   ◆

SANDY KOUFAX put together one of the most dominating stretches of pitching in baseball history. Over a five-year span, he led the NL in ERA five times and compiled a 111-34 record, before arthritis forced him to retire at age 30.

Sanford Koufax was born in Brooklyn in 1935, and while he liked baseball, he was very interested in basketball. In 1953, he went to the University of Cincinnati on a basketball scholarship. He also pitched for the baseball team. Late in 1954, he signed with his hometown Dodgers for $25,000.

Koufax started five games for the Dodgers in 1955, showing bursts of brilliance surrounded by intervals of wildness. His schooling continued for the next two seasons, when he got 10 and 13 starts and received much of his work out of the bullpen. The Dodgers moved to Los Angeles before the 1958 season, and Koufax posted an 11-11 mark with a 4.40 ERA in 26 starts and 40 appearances. He had 23 starts, an 8-6 mark, and a 4.05 ERA in 1959. He was 8-13 with a 3.91 ERA in 1960.

"Pitching is the art of instilling fear by making a man flinch."

—SANDY KOUFAX

In spring training of 1961, catcher Norm Sherry advised Koufax to slow his delivery, to throw changeups and curveballs, and to relax. Following that advice, Sandy recorded his first record over .500, going 18-13 and leading the league in Ks with the eye-popping total of 269. In 1962, Sandy developed a frightening numbness in his left index finger, due to a circulatory ailment. He was 14-7 with a league-leading 2.54 ERA that year, and pitched a no-hitter.

The 1963 season was his triumph. Sandy went 25-5, leading the NL with 25 wins, a 1.88 ERA, 11 shutouts, and 306 strikeouts. He won both the MVP and Cy Young Awards. He tossed his second no-hitter and won two games in the Dodgers' World Series victory. In 1964, he was 19-5 with a league-best 1.74 ERA. That year, a deteriorating arthritic condition in his left arm first became conspicuous. He continued to pitch with the help of cortisone shots and ice for two more seasons, winning Cy Young Awards in 1965 and '66. He had league-best ERAs of 2.04 and 1.73, and he won 26 and 27 games. He also tossed two more no-hitters, including a perfect game. He was inducted into the Hall of Fame in 1972.

MAJOR LEAGUE TOTALS										
W	L	ERA	G	CG	IP	H	ER	BB	SO
165	87	2.76	397	137	2,324.1	1,754	713	817	2,396

NAP LAJOIE

S E C O N D B A S E M A N

PHILADELPHIA PHILLIES 1896-1900
PHILADELPHIA ATHLETICS 1901-1902; 1915-1916
CLEVELAND BLUES (NAPS) 1902-1914

◆   ◆   ◆

THE CAREER of Napoleon Lajoie (1874-1959) got off to a rocky start. In 1896, Lajoie was purchased by the Philadelphia Phillies from the minors. By 1901, the Phils were pennant contenders. A salary hassle with Phillies owner Colonel Rogers, however, induced Lajoie to jump to the Philadelphia Athletics of the fledgling American League when A's manager Connie Mack offered a lucrative four-year pact.

Lajoie set a 20th century record by batting .422 and winning the AL Triple Crown in 1901, the league's first year. The smarting Phillies, however, obtained a state court injunction that prohibited Lajoie from playing with any other team in

Philadelphia. Since the injunction applied only in Pennsylvania, Mack traded Lajoie to Cleveland, for which he could play anywhere but in Philly. Due to the legal wrangling, Lajoie got into only 87 games in 1902, but he rebounded to lead the AL in hits in 1903 and 1904.

"If you pitched inside to [Lajoie], he'd tear the hand off the third baseman, and if you pitched outside he'd knock down the second baseman."

—ED WALSH

In all, Lajoie won three American League batting crowns, though his 1910 title is still disputed. Nap edged Ty Cobb by a single point after getting eight hits in a season-ending double-header, six of them bunts that Lajoie beat out as St. Louis Browns third baseman Red Corriden played deep to deny the hated Cobb the title.

Few of Lajoie's other accomplishments are tainted, however. For the first

13 years of the 20th century, he was the American League's Honus Wagner—the greatest fielder at his position of his time and also a great offensive player. Just the third man to collect 3,000 hits, Lajoie's lifetime average was .338.

Unlike Wagner, who played on four pennant winners in Pittsburgh, Lajoie was never on a championship team. Lajoie, who spent time as Cleveland's player-manager, was so popular that the team was renamed the "Naps" in his honor.

Although Lajoie stepped down as manager following the 1909 season, he remained with Cleveland five more seasons. He concluded his career with the A's and was elected to the Hall of Fame in 1936.

MAJOR LEAGUE TOTALS									
BA	G	AB	R	H	2B	3B	HR	RBI	SB
.338	2,479	9,592	1,503	3,244	658	161	83	1,599	382

BUCK LEONARD

FIRST BASEMAN

TEAMS INCLUDE: BALTIMORE STARS, BROOKLYN ROYAL GIANTS, HOMESTEAD GRAYS 1932-1950

◆　　　◆　　　◆

BUCK LEONARD was a left-handed, power-hitting first baseman who often drew comparisons to Lou Gehrig. Buck was a key ingredient to the domination of the Homestead Grays in the 1930s.

Walter Fenner Leonard (born in 1907) was born to a railroad fireman in Rocky Mount, North Carolina. Buck also worked on the railroad until the Depression forced him out of a job. He played semipro baseball with clubs in North Carolina and Virginia until 1933, when the Baltimore Stars signed him. He traveled with the team until it ran out of money in New York and disbanded. Stuck in New York, he was lucky to find a position with the Brooklyn Royal

Giants for the rest of the season. Leonard stopped in a New York bar owned by Joe Williams, a retired player who had starred on Cum Posey's Homestead Grays. Williams now had his eye open for talent, because the Grays had been all but wiped out by player raids and retirement.

"We never thought we'd get into the Hall of Fame. We thought the way we were playing was the way it was going to continue."

—BUCK LEONARD

Leonard had a tryout, and he signed to play first base for the Grays. The team began to regain respectability, and when Josh Gibson came aboard in 1937, the Grays caught fire, winning nine consecutive flags. And when Gibson jumped ship to play in Mexico in 1940, Leonard carried the club, hitting hit .392 in 1941 to lead the Negro National League. He had already won a pair of home run titles in his long career.

Buck was fairly well paid for his services. The Homestead Grays were based both in Pittsburgh and Washington, playing games in Forbes Field when the Pirates were out of town and in Griffith Stadium when the Senators were on the road. Since the Grays were able to fill both stadiums, they were able to pay their stars more than other Negro League teams. Leonard stayed with the Homestead Grays for his entire career, instead of jumping to other teams as other Negro League stars had done.

Leonard played in Mexico, Cuba, Puerto Rico, and Venezuela in the winter, and he also barnstormed with Satchel Paige's All-Stars. Buck played in Mexico in the early 1950s after he retired from the Grays. In 1972, Leonard was selected for the Hall of Fame.

NEGRO LEAGUE STATS*							
BA	G	AB	H	2B	3B	HR	SB
.324	382	1,587	514	85	33	71	10

Note: Leonard's Negro League stats are incomplete.

POP LLOYD
SHORTSTOP
FIRST BASEMAN
CATCHER
MANAGER

TEAMS INCLUDE: MACON ACMES, CUBAN X-GIANTS, BROOKLYN ROYAL GIANTS, PHILADELPHIA GIANTS, LELAND GIANTS, NEW YORK LINCOLN GIANTS, CHICAGO AMERICAN GIANTS, COLUMBUS BUCKEYES, ATLANTIC CITY BACHARACH GIANTS, PHILADELPHIA HILLDALES, NEW YORK HARLEM STARS 1905-1932

◆　　　◆　　　◆

POP LLOYD first jumped from semipro baseball to the black professional leagues in 1905 at age 21, and he was a good enough player to play semipro until he was age 58. He was a very good defensive shortstop for much of his career, and he showcased a line-drive stroke that drove his average to dizzying heights.

Born in northeast Florida, John Henry Lloyd (1884-1964) started playing semipro ball in the mid-1910s. Moving to the Cuban X-Giants in 1905, Pop began his career as a catcher. By 1907, he was a shortstop and a cleanup hitter. Lloyd played for whatever team could pay him. He spent time on various Philadelphia teams, on New York and New Jersey teams, and with the Chicago American Giants, among others.

No less than Babe Ruth said that Lloyd was the greatest ballplayer he had ever seen.

In a 1910 12-game exhibition series in Cuba against the Detroit Tigers, Lloyd went 11-for-22. While the Bengals won seven games, Ty Cobb (who batted .370) was sufficiently embarrassed to vow never to play against blacks again. In 1914, Rube Foster enticed Pop to play for the Chicago American Giants. In the Windy City he teamed with "Home Run" Johnson in a legendary double-play combination.

Lloyd was often likened to Honus Wagner, a comparison Wagner was proud to acknowledge. It was an apt analogy, because like Honus, Lloyd was highly regarded, was a terrific hitter, and was known to scoop up dirt and pebbles along with ground balls.

At age 44 in 1928, still in the pros, Pop hit .564 in 37 games, with 11 homers and 10 steals. The next year, he hit .388. Pitcher Sam Streeter said, "Everything he hit was just like you were hanging out clothes on a line." Not only was Pop a great hitter, but he had an intimate knowledge of the game. In 1915, Lloyd had the first of many stints as a player-manager, and in 1921 he took charge of the short-lived Columbus, Ohio, franchise in Rube Foster's new Black National League. It was there that he finally acquired his nickname. Pop was named to the Hall of Fame in 1977.

NEGRO LEAGUE STATS*							
BA	G	AB	H	2B	3B	HR	SB
.368	477	1,769	651	90	18	26	56

*Note: Lloyd's stats are games that were recorded from 1914 to 1932 only. His career stats are incomplete.

GREG MADDUX

PITCHER

CHICAGO CUBS 1986-1992
ATLANTA BRAVES 1993-1996

◆ ◆ ◆

GREG MADDUX was the first pitcher
in baseball history to win four consecutive Cy Young Awards, and he accomplished the feat in two of the best hitters'
parks of his time, Wrigley Field in Chicago
and "The Launching Pad," Fulton County
Stadium in Atlanta.

Gregory Alan Maddux (born in 1966)
grew up in Las Vegas and was a Nevada
all-state pitcher in his junior and senior
seasons in high school. He was a second-
round pick by the Cubs in 1984, and he
made the big-league roster by 1986.

A full-time starter by 1987, Maddux
was 6-14 with a 5.61 ERA. Though he was
young at that point, Maddux wasn't big

(6', 175 pounds) and didn't have an over-powering fastball, so there wasn't much hope of him becoming a top hurler.

"That's more than the Clinton administration is spending on arms."
—DON MCMILLAN ON THE BRAVES' EXPENSIVE STARTING ROTATION OF GREG MADDUX, TOM GLAVINE, JOHN SMOLTZ, AND STEVE AVERY

Yet it didn't take "Mad Dog" long to become one of the best pitchers in the National League. The next season, he was 15-3 by the All-Star break and was the youngest Cub in history to be named to the All-Star team. After following up his surprising 1988 season with three quality years, in 1992 he won his first of four straight Cy Young Awards, going 20-11 with a 2.18 ERA, 199 strikeouts, and 70 walks allowed in 268 innings of work. The numbers were remarkable, and Maddux entered free agency following the season.

After flirting with several teams, Mad-dux signed a $28 million, five-year contract with Atlanta, joining with Tom Glavine, John Smoltz, Steve Avery, and others to form the deepest starting rotation in baseball since the early 1970s Orioles. The Atlanta pitching staff combined with a top everyday lineup to consistently make the playoffs in the 1990s, and the team won the World Series in 1995.

Maddux started proving that he was worth all that money in 1993, notching a 20-10 record with a 2.36 ERA, winning a second Cy Young. He cut his walks allowed to 52 with 197 strikeouts in 267 innings. In the strike-shortened 1994 season, he went 16-6 with a phenomenal 1.56 ERA and 156 Ks and 31 walks in 202 innings, garnering Cy Young No. 3. For No. 4 in 1995, he went 19-2 with a 1.63 ERA. He cut his walks allowed to 23 while garnering 181 strikeouts.

MAJOR LEAGUE TOTALS									
W	L	ERA	G	CG	IP	H	ER	BB	SO
165	104	2.86	336	75	2,365.2	2,102	753	589	1,643

MICKEY MANTLE

O U T F I E L D E R

NEW YORK YANKEES 1951-1968

◆   ◆   ◆

MICKEY MANTLE was the most
feared hitter on the most successful team in history, and he overcame great
pain in his quest to satisfy his fans, his
father, and himself.

Mickey Charles Mantle (1931-1995)
was born in Spavinaw, Oklahoma, the son
of Mutt Mantle, a lead miner who had
dreams of a good life for Mickey. Mickey
(named after Mickey Cochrane) was a
standout schoolboy player, but a serious
football injury nearly derailed his career—
and his life. He suffered from osteo-
myelitis, a condition that weakened his left
leg, and may have lost the leg if his mother
had not procured a then-new treatment
with a revolutionary drug, penicillin.

The Yankees signed Mickey to a contract in 1949, and in two minor-league seasons he hit well but struggled at shortstop. As a rookie for New York in 1951, he played right field. He replaced Joe Dimaggio in center in '52. In his best seasons, and there were many, Mantle was simply a devastating player. He could run like the wind and hit tape-measure homers, like his famous 565-footer in Washington in 1953. He led the Yanks to 12 fall classics in 14 years, and seven world championships. He set records for most homers, RBI, runs, walks, and strikeouts in World Series play. He led the AL with 129 runs in 1954, and got his first home run title in 1955 with 37. He was a free-swinger who struck out often, but could also take a walk, drawing at least 100 10 times.

In 1956, Mantle had one of the greatest seasons ever at bat. He hit 52 homers with 130 RBI and a .353 average to win the Triple Crown. He also led the league with 132 runs and a .705 slugging percentage.

He had 112 walks and won the first of three Most Valuable Player Awards. He won the MVP in 1957, hitting .365 with 34 homers, 94 RBI, 121 runs, and 146 walks.

Mantle notched homer crowns in 1958 and 1960, then got into a duel with Roger Maris in 1961 to break Babe Ruth's single-season home run mark. While Maris's 61 was the winner, Mick led the league with a .687 slugging percentage, 132 runs scored, and 126 bases on balls. Mick won an MVP Award in 1962 with a .321 average, 20 homers, and 89 RBI.

"[Mantle] was the best one-legged player I ever saw play the game."

—CASEY STENGEL

Mantle's high school leg injury, torn knee cartilage in 1951, and many other injuries he suffered after that shortened his career and were a constant hindrance. After two painful seasons in 1967 and 1968, The Mick retired. Despite his ailments, he had hit 536 home runs.

As the 1980s progressed, Mantle's alcoholism, which had been bad during his playing days, worsened. By the 1990s, he had sought treatment for the illness, but damage had already been done to his body. Early in 1995, he was diagnosed with cancer and received a liver transplant. "The Mick" used the publicity from his hospitalization to urge his fans to register for organ donation programs and to stay away from drugs and alcohol, saying, "God gave me a body and the ability to play baseball. . . . I just wasted it." The cancer spread to different parts of Mantle's body, and he died on August 13, 1995. His passing was mourned by a generation of fans who never forgot what a truly great player he was.

MAJOR LEAGUE TOTALS									
BA	G	AB	R	H	2B	3B	HR	RBI	SB
.298	2,401	8,102	1,677	2,415	344	72	536	1,509	153

JUAN MARICHAL

P I T C H E R

SAN FRANCISCO GIANTS 1960-1973
BOSTON RED SOX 1974
LOS ANGELES DODGERS 1975

◆　　　◆　　　◆

JUAN MARICHAL won more games,
191, than any pitcher during the 1960s.
He was a good strikeout pitcher, but also
the greatest control artist of his time,
walking just 709 men in more than 3,500
innings. His delivery defied logic. The tim-
ing oddities and whirl of motion that
resulted from his high-kick windup baffled
hitters for 16 seasons.

Dominican Republic native Juan Anto-
nio Marichal y Sanchez (born in 1937)
signed with the Giants in 1958 and led the
Midwest League with 21 wins and a 1.87
ERA. Marichal paced the Eastern League
in '59 with 18 wins and a 2.39 ERA, and

was 11-5 the next year in the Pacific Coast League.

Called to San Francisco in mid-1960, Marichal went 6-2 with a 2.66 ERA. In 1963, Marichal led the NL with 25 wins and pitched a no-hitter. He also bested Warren Spahn in a 16-inning complete-game win. This was the first of six 20-win seasons in seven years for "Manito," and each season his ERA was under 3.00.

Marichal won 154 games during the seven-year period from 1963 to 1969, including three seasons of 25 or more victories.

On August 22, 1965, Marichal batted against Sandy Koufax. Juan had thrown a few brushback pitches, and when Dodger receiver John Roseboro asked Koufax to retaliate, Sandy refused. Marichal, thinking Roseboro's throws to Koufax ticked his ear, slugged the catcher several times with his bat. A vicious fight ensued.

Marichal was suspended and fined, and since the Giants finished just two games back of the flag-winning Dodgers, his absence was costly.

In his first major-league start, in 1960, Marichal held the Phillies hitless until the eighth inning.

The incident may have kept Marichal, who was 243-142 lifetime, from ever winning a Cy Young Award, and he did not make the Hall of Fame until 1983. Perhaps the best right-hander of the 1960s, he finished in the top three in wins five times and ERA three times. He feasted on the Dodgers, beating them in 37 of 55 decisions. Ironically, he spent 1975, his last season, with Los Angeles. "The Dominican Dandy" compiled a lifetime 2.89 ERA.

MAJOR LEAGUE TOTALS									
W	L	ERA	G	CG	IP	H	ER	BB	SO
243	142	2.89	471	244	3,509.1	3,153	1,126	709	2,303

EDDIE MATHEWS

BOSTON BRAVES 1952
MILWAUKEE BRAVES 1953-1965
ATLANTA BRAVES 1966
HOUSTON ASTROS 1967
DETROIT TIGERS 1967-1968

◆   ◆   ◆

EDDIE MATHEWS teamed with Hank Aaron to form a lethal one-two punch in the 1950s and early 1960s. Mathews, who hit 512 career homers, was the best-hitting third baseman in history before Mike Schmidt.

Edwin Lee Mathews (born in 1931) was pursued by the Brooklyn Dodgers, who offered a $10,000 contract. He was also courted by the Boston Braves, who offered $6,000. Eddie decided that signing with Boston would give him the best opportunity to move to the majors quickly.

Mathews batted .363 with 17 homers in 1949, his first pro season, and slugged 32 homers the next year in the Southern League.

Mathews was promoted to Boston in 1952, and though he led the NL in strikeouts, he cracked 25 homers. The next year, the Braves left for Milwaukee and Mathews's 47 round-trippers led the NL. He notched 37 or more taters and 95 or more RBI from 1954 to '56.

"I'd made better plays, but that big one in the spotlight stamped me the way I wanted to be remembered."

—EDDIE MATHEWS ON THE DIVING STOP HE MADE TO END THE 1957 WORLD SERIES

In 1957, he batted .292 with 32 homers and 94 RBI as the Braves won a world championship. He hit just .251 with 31 four-baggers as the Braves won another pennant in 1958, but Eddie won the homer crown in 1959 with 46 dingers.

Mathews hit at least 30 homers in nine

seasons, setting a National League record. Four times he hit more than 40. He led the league in walks four times and scored at least 95 runs in 10 straight seasons. While Henry Aaron and Mathews played together, they hit 863 home runs, more than Babe Ruth and Lou Gehrig slugged as teammates.

Mathews, initially a poor defensive player, eventually became a capable third baseman. He led the NL in putouts twice and assists three times. He is among the top third sackers in career double plays.

In 1962, Mathews injured his shoulder, and his ability gradually declined. After one year in Atlanta in 1966, he was traded to Houston and later to Detroit before retiring in 1968. Mathews was elected to baseball's Hall of Fame in 1978.

MAJOR LEAGUE TOTALS									
BA	G	AB	R	H	2B	3B	HR	RBI	SB
.271	2,388	8,537	1,509	2,315	354	72	512	1,453	68

CHRISTY MATHEWSON

PITCHER

NEW YORK GIANTS 1900-1916
CINCINNATI REDS 1916

◆　　　◆　　　◆

CHRISTY MATHEWSON left Bucknell University in 1899 to sign his first baseball contract. Seventeen years later, he retired with 373 victories and an almost universal recognition as the greatest pitcher in National League history.

Christopher Mathewson (1880-1925) probably did more than any other performer of his day to enhance the image of a professional baseball player. Educated, intelligent, and a consummate gentleman, he seemed almost too good to be true.

After winning 20 games as a rookie for the New York Giants in 1901, Matty tumbled to just 14 victories the next year. After that, however, he reeled off 12 straight seasons in which he won 20 or more games. "Big Six" won more than 30 games on four occasions with a high of 37 in 1908. The net result of his extraordinary run of success was that he had 300 career victories by the time he was 32 years old.

"You can learn little from victory. You can learn everything from defeat."
—CHRISTY MATHEWSON

Sometimes, though, Mathewson seemed to have trouble winning the big games. In his last three World Series appearances—1911, 1912, and 1913—Matty won just two games while losing five. In his defense, the Giants consistently displayed defensive lapses at crucial moments when he was on the mound and scored only seven runs in the last 39 innings he hurled in Series play.

However, Mathewson's work in championship contests did not always end in disappointment. In 1905, his first World Series appearance, he twirled a record three shutouts and 27 scoreless innings against the Philadelphia Athletics to lead the Giants to victory in their first 20th century postseason affair. Matty's feat is considered by many to be the most outstanding performance in World Series history.

In 1916, with his famed screwball, or "fadeaway," no longer effective, Mathewson was traded to Cincinnati so that he could become the Reds' player-manager. After only one mound appearance in the Queen City, he became a bench pilot only. In 1918, Matty entered the Army in August. While serving overseas in World War I, he accidentally inhaled poison gas, permanently damaging his lungs. He died on October 7, 1925. In 1936, Christy was among the first group of five players elected to the Hall of Fame.

MAJOR LEAGUE TOTALS									
W	L	ERA	G	CG	IP	H	ER	BB	SO
373	188	2.13	634	435	4,782.0	2,502	1,132	838	2,502

WILLIE MAYS

OUTFIELDER

NEW YORK GIANTS 1951-1952; 1954-1957
SAN FRANCISCO GIANTS 1958-1972
NEW YORK METS 1972-1973

◆   ◆   ◆

FEW PLAYERS have combined grace, popularity, and accomplishment like Willie Mays. He was a beautiful defensive outfielder, a tremendous power hitter, an outstanding thrower, a canny baserunner, a huge drawing card, and a durable champion.

Born in 1931 in Westfield, Alabama, Willie Howard Mays was so advanced that he competed with the men on his father's steel mill team when Willie was 14 years old. He was one of the last players, and likely the best, to go from the Negro Leagues to the big leagues. In 1950, the Giants signed him and sent him to the Inter-State League, where he batted .353. In 1951, he was batting .477 at Minneapolis of the American Association when the Giants promoted him.

Although Willie started out 0-for-12, he had a galvanizing effect on the Giants. They came from 13½ games back to force a playoff with the front-running Dodgers, beating them on Bobby Thomson's home run. Mays hit 20 homers, perfected center field play, and won the Rookie of the Year Award. He also won the hearts of teammates and fans alike for his enthusiasm, good humor, squeaky voice, and incredible play. Manager Leo Durocher said, "What can I say about Willie Mays after I say he's the greatest player any of us has ever seen?"

Mays was in the Army for most of 1952 and all of 1953. If he had played in those years, he almost certainly would have broken Babe Ruth's lifetime home run record. In 1954, Willie returned to win the MVP Award; he led the league with a .345 average and a .667 slugging percentage, and he hit 41 homers. His catch of a Vic Wertz drive in the Giants' World Series victory has become one of baseball's most admired moments.

Willie led the NL in homers with 51 in 1955. He hit more than 35 homers in each of 11 seasons, hit 40 homers six times (twice topping 50), and won five slugging crowns. In addition to his power, average, arm, and defense, add speed; he won four stolen base and three triples titles. His biggest victory came over the skeptical San Francisco fans. When the Giants moved out to the West Coast in 1958, Willie melted all resistance with his spectacular play.

The 1962 campaign was one of Willie's best seasons, as he hit 49 homers and drove in 141 runs. In 1965, he won his second MVP by batting .317 with 52 homers and 112 RBI. Mays finished among the top six in MVP voting 12 times.

Mays won a dozen Gold Gloves in a row, from 1957 to 1968. Mickey Mantle, the man Mays would be compared to most often, said, "You have to work hard to be able to make things look as easy as Willie makes them look." Willie retired with records for games, putouts, and chances for center fielders.

"It isn't hard to be good from time to time in sports. What's tough is being good every day."

—WILLIE MAYS

Willie Mays, the "Say Hey Kid," showed true greatness in his longevity. At age 40, he led the league in walks, hit 18 homers, and was 23-for-26 as a basestealer. He spent his final two seasons back with the New Yorkers who missed him, with the Mets, and appeared in one final World Series. He was a near-unanimous selection to the Hall of Fame in 1979.

MAJOR LEAGUE TOTALS									
BA	G	AB	R	H	2B	3B	HR	RBI	SB
.302	2,992	10,881	2,062	3,283	523	140	660	1,903	338

WILLIE McCOVEY

FIRST BASEMAN

SAN FRANCISCO GIANTS 1959-1973; 1977-1980
SAN DIEGO PADRES 1974-1976
OAKLAND ATHLETICS 1976

◆　　　◆　　　◆

WHILE WILLIE MAYS was a super-star known around the world, the "other" Willie on the 1960s San Francisco Giants was one of the great sluggers of the decade, averaging 30 homers a year and leading the league in round-trippers three times.

Willie Lee McCovey (born in 1938) was signed by the Giants in 1955, and prompt-ly led the Georgia State League with 113 RBI. In 1958, Willie hit .319 with 89 RBI in the Pacific Coast League. Unfortunately, the Giants had 1958 Rookie of the Year Orlando Cepeda at first base. After McCovey hit .372 with 29 homers in 95

PCL games in 1959, he went to San Francisco and belted 13 homers with a .354 average in 52 games to himself become Rookie of the Year.

"I'd walk me."
—WILLIE MCCOVEY, ON HOW HE WOULD PITCH TO
WILLIE MCCOVEY

In 1960, however, McCovey slumped and returned to the minors. In 1961 and 1962, he hit 38 four-baggers in half-time play for the Giants before winning an everyday job in 1963. "Stretch" promptly led the league with 44 home runs, but slumped due to injuries in 1964.

The Giants reached the World Series in 1962. In the ninth inning of the seventh game, McCovey, with the tying and winning runs on, lined out—"the hardest ball I ever hit," according to Stretch—straight to second base.

McCovey won the National League MVP Award in 1969, pacing the loop with 45 homers and 126 RBI. He led the circuit in slugging percentage in 1967, 1968, and 1969. After a .289 average and 39 homers in 1970, he missed much of the next two years with various ailments.

In 1969, McCovey received a major-league-record 45 intentional walks.

The popular but aging and injury-prone McCovey was traded to the Padres in 1974. In 1977, he returned to the Giants, and batted .280 with 28 homers to win the National League Comeback Player of the Year Award. He is tied with Ted Williams with 521 career home runs. McCovey was named to the Hall of Fame in 1986.

			MAJOR LEAGUE TOTALS						
BA	G	AB	R	H	2B	3B	HR	RBI	SB
.270	2,588	8,197	1,229	2,211	353	46	521	1,550	26

JOHNNY MIZE

FIRST BASEMAN

ST. LOUIS CARDINALS 1936-1941
NEW YORK GIANTS 1942; 1946-1949
NEW YORK YANKEES 1949-1953

◆   ◆   ◆

HARD-HITTING first baseman Johnny Mize, who led the National League in homers four times, linked the great 1930s Cardinal teams to the Yankee dynasty of the 1950s.

John Robert Mize (1913-1993) of Demorest, Georgia, signed with Greensboro of the Piedmont League while still in high school. In 1933, while in the International League, Mize was purchased by the St. Louis Cardinals.

Mize joined the Cards in 1936 and batted .329 with 19 home runs. He developed his power and also hit .300 for the next eight seasons, peaking at .364 in 1937. In 1939, Johnny led the league in homers and batting average. In 1940, his 43 dingers topped the NL, and his 137 RBI also led the league. Mize paced the NL in slugging percentage annually between 1938 and 1940. He hit .312 lifetime, walked around 75 times a season, and rarely struck out.

> *"Your arm is gone; your legs likewise. But not your eyes, Mize, not your eyes."*
>
> —DAN PARKER

Traded to the New York Giants, Mize led the National League in 1942 with a .521 slugging percentage and 110 RBI. He served three years in the Navy, but returned in 1946 to top the National League twice more in home runs. His 51 round-trippers in 1947 are still an NL lefty record. He also paced the loop in RBI and runs scored.

Late in the 1949 pennant drive, the Yankees acquired Mize for $40,000. After pounding 25 homers in just 274 at bats in 1950, Mize was the hero of the 1952 World

Series. He hit .400 with three homers, grabbing Series MVP honors. Johnny led the American League in pinch hits from 1951 to '53.

"The Big Cat" won five World Series rings with the powerful Yanks. He retired after the 1953 season. The first slugger in history to hit three home runs in a game six times, Mize was named to the Hall of Fame in 1981.

			MAJOR LEAGUE TOTALS						
BA	G	AB	R	H	2B	3B	HR	RBI	SB
.312	1,884	6,443	1,118	2,011	367	83	359	1,337	28

JOE MORGAN

SECOND BASEMAN

HOUSTON ASTROS 1963-1971; 1980
CINCINNATI REDS 1972-1979
SAN FRANCISCO GIANTS 1981-1982
PHILADELPHIA PHILLIES 1983
OAKLAND ATHLETICS 1984

◆   ◆   ◆

L ITTLE JOE made the Big Red Machine go. Joe Morgan is best remembered for being a catalyst for the world champion Reds in 1975 and 1976. He also played more games at second base than anyone but Eddie Collins.

Joe Leonard Morgan was born in 1943 in Bonham, Texas. After attending the same high school that produced Frank Robinson, Morgan signed with the Astros in 1963. In 1964, he was the Texas League MVP, batting .319 with 42 doubles, 12 homers, and 90 RBI.

In 1965, Morgan was the Houston second baseman. Houston coach Nellie Fox taught Joe a "chicken flap" of his left elbow while taking his batting stance, to remind him to keep his elbow high. The 5'7" second baseman scored 100 runs and was Rookie of the Year runner-up. Though a productive second baseman with Houston for seven years, Morgan didn't reach the limelight until he was traded to Cincinnati in 1972.

"[Morgan] has the conviction that he should affect the outcome of every game he plays in every time he comes up to bat and every time he gets on base."

—ROGER ANGELL

Finally out of the Astrodome, Morgan hit 16 homers in 1972, 26 in '73, and 22 in 1974. His walk totals those three years were 115, 111, and 120, and he scored 122, 116, and 107 runs.

Morgan was the first second baseman in baseball history to win back-to-back

MVP Awards, in 1975 and '76. In 1975, he batted .327 with 17 homers, 107 runs scored, 94 RBI, 67 stolen bases, and a league-best 132 bases on balls as the Reds won 108 games. Morgan batted .320 with 27 homers, 113 runs scored, 111 RBI, 60 swipes, and 114 walks in 1976.

Joe was a steady fielder and won five straight Gold Gloves from 1973 to '77. He led the Reds to another playoff berth in 1979. He then moved back to Houston in 1980, again appearing in the NLCS. In 1983, he joined the Phillies and appeared in his last World Series.

Joe led the NL in walks four times and runs once. He never led the circuit in stolen bases, but he finished in the top three eight times. Joe was elected to the Hall of Fame in 1990.

MAJOR LEAGUE TOTALS									
BA	G	AB	R	H	2B	3B	HR	RBI	SB
.271	2,649	9,277	1,650	2,517	449	96	268	1,133	689

EDDIE MURRAY

FIRST BASEMAN

BALTIMORE ORIOLES 1977-1988; 1996
LOS ANGELES DODGERS 1989-1991
NEW YORK METS 1992-1993
CLEVELAND INDIANS 1994-1996

◆   ◆   ◆

S TRONG, DEPENDABLE Eddie Murray averaged 28 homers each of his first 12 seasons as a Baltimore Oriole from 1977 to 1988, and drove in at least 76 runs every year during that stretch.

Standards of excellence were set early for Eddie Clarence Murray (born in 1956), who played high school baseball in Los Angeles with future major-leaguers Ozzie Smith and Darrell Jackson. A third-round pick by the Orioles in 1973, Murray made three minor-league All-Star teams.

A natural right-hander, Murray taught himself to switch-hit. In 1977 at age 21, he broke into the big leagues with style, becoming the fourth Oriole to capture AL Rookie of the Year honors. Murray was also the first major-league player to win the trophy while appearing mostly as a designated hitter.

In 1996, Murray set a major-league record by notching his 20th consecutive season with 75 or more RBI.

Placed at first base in 1978, Murray continued his excellent production at bat while thriving in the field. He won three straight Gold Gloves, from 1982 to '84, and was among the best at fielding bunts and gaining force-outs at second base.

Murray continued to improve at bat, and in 1983 posted then-career highs in home runs, runs, and walks. Eddie led the Orioles to a resounding victory over the Phillies in the 1983 World Series.

Except for the 1981 strike year, he had at least 84 RBI per season each of his 12

Oriole campaigns. He continued to produce after his days in Baltimore, hitting .330 with the 1991 Dodgers and smacking 27 homers for the 1993 Mets. Murray moved to Cleveland in 1994. On June 30, 1995, he garnered his 3,000th hit against Minnesota's Mike Trombley. Despite suffering broken ribs in a home plate collision, he batted .323 with 21 homers to help the Indians reach their first World Series in 47 years. Back in Baltimore in 1996, he became the third major-leaguer, after Willie Mays and Hank Aaron, to notch 3,000 career hits and 500 career homers.

Murray's involvement in community work led to nominations for the Roberto Clemente Humanitarian Award in 1984 and '85 for his sponsoring of medical, educational, and religious foundations.

MAJOR LEAGUE TOTALS									
BA	G	AB	R	H	2B	3B	HR	RBI	SB
.288	2,971	11,169	1,614	3,218	553	35	501	1,899	109

STAN MUSIAL

ST. LOUIS CARDINALS 1941-1944; 1946-1963

◆　　　◆　　　◆

Stan "THE MAN" MUSIAL starred for
the St. Louis Cardinals for 22 seasons
and was the first National League player to
win three Most Valuable Player Awards.

Stanley Frank Musial was born in 1920
in Donora, Pennsylvania. When Musial
was a youngster he was the batboy for a
local team, until they gave him the opportunity to pitch and he rang up 13 Ks in six
innings. When he was just 18 years old,
Musial joined the Cardinals organization
as a pitcher.

Assigned to Daytona Beach in the
Florida State League in 1940, Stan was
pitching very well and hitting over .300.
Musial injured his pitching arm, but the
Cards, aware of his great athletic talent,
moved him to the outfield full-time. He

performed so well that he was in the majors by the end of 1941.

In 1942, the emerging Cardinal powerhouse won the first of three straight pennants and the World Series as the rookie Musial hit .315. In 1943, he won his first MVP Award, leading the league with a .357 batting average, 220 base hits, 48 doubles, and 20 triples. He again led the NL in hits and doubles in 1944.

Musial had good home run power, terrific doubles power, and, for his time, was a spectacular triples hitter. He was terrifically fast—one of his nicknames was "The Donora Greyhound"—and was a fine fielder, in left field and later as a first baseman. Though he never led the league in homers, he won six slugging titles and in 1954 hit five round-trippers in a double-header. His unique corkscrew batting stance, described by Ted Lyons as "like a kid peeking around the corner to see if the cops are coming," resulted in seven batting crowns. He posted a lifetime .416 on-base average, scoring at least 105 runs in 11 straight seasons.

> *"A couple of years ago they told me I was too young to be President and you were too old to be playing baseball, but we both fooled them."*
>
> —THE 45-YEAR-OLD JOHN F. KENNEDY TO THE 42-YEAR-OLD STAN MUSIAL AT THE 1962 ALL-STAR GAME

In the Navy in 1945, Stan the Man came back to win his second MVP in 1946 as the Cards won another world championship. He led the league with a .365 batting average, 50 doubles, 20 triples, and 124 runs scored. He won his third Most Valuable Player trophy in 1948. He missed the Triple Crown by a single home run, hitting a career-high 39 to Johnny Mize's and Ralph Kiner's 40. Musial had a .376 average (the NL's highest since Bill Terry hit .401 in 1930), 230 base hits, 46 doubles, 18 triples, 131 RBI, and 135 runs, all of which led the NL. Aside from his three MVPs, Stan finished second four times.

Several of the other NL organizations gained ground on St. Louis and its farm system by the early 1950s. Stan won batting crowns from 1950 to 1952 (with averages of .346, .355, and .336), but the Cardinals could finish no better than third. Stan won his final batting title in 1957 when he was age 37, and the Redbirds finished second. But while Stan maintained his excellence, St. Louis from 1953 to '59 would get no closer than fourth place or 17 games out at the end.

Musial hit .330 in 1962, when he was 42 years old. In his final season, 1963, he hit a home run in his first at bat after becoming a grandfather. Musial was voted the Player of the Decade in 1956 for the period from 1946 to 1955. Stan the Man was elected to the Hall of Fame in 1969.

MAJOR LEAGUE TOTALS									
BA	G	AB	R	H	2B	3B	HR	RBI	SB
.331	3,026	10,972	1,949	3,630	725	177	475	1,951	78

KID NICHOLS

P I T C H E R

BOSTON BEANEATERS 1890-1901
ST. LOUIS CARDINALS 1904-1905
PHILADELPHIA PHILLIES 1905-1906

◆　　　◆　　　◆

WHEN HE FIRST JOINED the Boston Beaneaters in 1890, Charlie Augustus Nichols looked so youthful and unprepossessing that he was called "Kid." The nickname stuck with him for the remainder of his 14-year big-league career, during which he won 361 games—including 297 during the 1890s, more than any other pitcher in any decade.

Nichols (1869-1953) began his career in 1887 with his hometown Kansas City club in the Western League. After two seasons, Nichols landed with Omaha in the Western Association. Frank Selee, Omaha's manager, was hired to skipper the Boston Beaneaters the next year and brought Nichols with him.

Kid Nichols is the only 300-game winner in major-league history who got by with just a fastball (and a none-too-overpowering fastball at that). What Nichols had in spades was control. When he walked a batter, it was usually because he preferred not to let him hit.

In 1900, Nichols became the youngest pitcher ever to win 300 games, a distinction he still holds.

Nichols won 30 or more games eight times for Boston, reaching a high of 35 in 1892. Five years he pitched more than 400 innings, and more than 300 in 11. Never a strikeout or ERA leader, Kid nevertheless topped the National League three times in shutouts and always ranked among the leaders in complete games and saves (staff aces were also used in relief back then).

The 1890s Beaneaters were baseball's premier team, largely due to Nichols.

However, team owner Arthur Soden lost several of his stars in the early 1900s when he refused to match offers made to them by new American League clubs. Nichols quit the Beaneaters and bought a share of the Kansas City team in the Western League.

Nichols holds the major-league record for most wins in a decade, having won 297 decisions in the 1890s.

After two years as a player-manager with Kansas City, Kid was lured back to the majors by the St. Louis Cardinals, who offered him the same dual role. He won 21 games for St. Louis in 1904 and finished his career with the Phillies two years later. At age 36, Nichols had tossed more than 5,000 innings in 582 games. Nichols was named to the Hall of Fame in 1949.

MAJOR LEAGUE TOTALS									
W	L	ERA	G	CG	IP	H	ER	BB	SO
361	208	2.94	620	532	5,084	4,912	1,661	1,272	1,877

MEL OTT

NEW YORK GIANTS 1926-1947

◆　　　◆　　　◆

MEL OTT stood out even in an era of great sluggers for his youth, his odd batting stance, and his great performance over nearly two decades.

Melvin Thomas Ott (1909-1958) of Gretna, Louisiana, was a three-sport high school star. He played semipro ball at age 16 for a team with connections to John McGraw.

McGraw himself eventually gave Ott a tryout. Impressed with his hitting ability, even though Mel had an unorthodox batting technique, McGraw signed Ott but refused to send him to the minors, fearing a farm skipper would alter Ott's stance and thus "ruin" him.

Ott's stance was certainly unique. He lifted his front foot before swinging, his hands held almost below his belt. The result was a level swing with terrific power, amply announced by 42 home runs and 152 RBI in 1929, his second full year.

"Every time I sign a ball, I thank my luck that I wasn't born Coveleski or Wambsganss or Peckinpaugh."

—MEL OTT

He also led the league in 1929 with 113 walks, a sign of the discipline that would lead to a lifetime on-base average of .410. He was just 20 years old, and his boyish appearance and size (5'7") reinforced the impression of youth that stayed with him throughout his career. In fact, Ott made the Hall of Fame when he was just 42.

Ott was a fine outfielder with a great arm, leading NL outfielders in double plays in 1929 and 1935. He benefited greatly from his home park, hitting just 187 of his 511 homers on the road. Mel was a World Series hero in 1933, hitting

.389 with two homers, one winning the final game in the 10th inning.

Ott set an NL record in 1926 as the youngest player to ever get a pinch hit, at age 17. In 1929, he set a major-league mark as the youngest player to ever hit 40 homers, at age 20.

Ott became player-manager of the Giants in 1942 but failed to win a pennant. Known for his sweet disposition, he was also a taskmaster as a manager, and helped the careers of such players as Johnny Mize. A 1958 car crash took Ott from this world too soon.

MAJOR LEAGUE TOTALS									
BA	G	AB	R	H	2B	3B	HR	RBI	SB
.304	2,734	9,456	1,859	2,876	488	72	511	1,861	89

SATCHEL
PAIGE

P I T C H E R

NEGRO LEAGUE TEAMS INCLUDE: CHATTANOOGA BLACK LOOKOUTS, BIRMINGHAM BLACK BARONS, NASHVILLE ELITE GIANTS, CLEVELAND CUBS, PITTSBURGH CRAWFORDS, KANSAS CITY MONARCHS' "B" TEAM, KANSAS CITY MONARCHS, ST. LOUIS STARS, PHILADELPHIA STARS 1926-1947; 1950

MAJOR LEAGUE TEAMS:
CLEVELAND INDIANS 1948-1949
ST. LOUIS BROWNS 1951-1953
KANSAS CITY ATHLETICS 1965

◆   ◆   ◆

SOMETIMES IT SEEMS that Satchel Paige was more a mythological being than a flesh-and-blood man. He was the most popular baseball player in the Negro Leagues. He was ageless and could do anything with a baseball.

Leroy Robert Paige (1906-1982) was born in Mobile, Alabama, one of 11 children. He was signed by the semipro Mobile Tigers in 1924, and by 1926 he was hurling for the Chattanooga Black Lookouts. He jumped to the Birmingham Black Barons in 1927, all the while pitching exhibition games and in the Caribbean and Mexico in the winter. He stayed with Birmingham until 1930.

Paige had two fastballs that were overpowering: "Long Tommy," which was supersonic, and "Little Tommy," which was merely unhittable. He also threw his "bee ball," named because it would "be where I want it to be."

Paige gained fame when he joined the Pittsburgh Crawfords in the early 1930s, with batterymate Josh Gibson and a host of other stars. When Paige barnstormed around the country or pitched in the Dominican Republic, he was so popular that fans would not come to see his teams unless he pitched, so he would pitch every day. He also regularly got the best of the likes of Dizzy Dean and Bob Feller.

When his arm wore down late in his career, Paige used several hesitation deliveries that were so convincing that hitters were helpless. When his arm recovered in 1939, he was a better pitcher than he had been in the 1930s. Satchel pitched for the Monarchs in the 1940s, but he was more an independent operator than a team member.

Finally, in 1948, Cleveland Browns owner Bill Veeck signed Paige to a contract. Paige was 6-1, pitching before packed houses, as the Browns won the pennant. Paige's last big-league appearance came in 1965 at age 59. He continued to pitch well in the minor leagues for years. Paige was inducted into the Hall of Fame in 1971.

NEGRO LEAGUE STATS*

W	L	G	CG	IP	H	BB	SO
123	79	279	122	1,584	1,142	241	1,177

*Note: Paige's Negro League career stats are incomplete.

MAJOR LEAGUE TOTALS

W	L	ERA	G	CG	IP	H	ER	BB	SO
28	31	3.29	179	7	476.0	429	174	183	290

JIM PALMER

PITCHER

BALTIMORE ORIOLES 1965-1967; 1969-1984

◆ ◆ ◆

THE IMAGE of Jim Palmer as a sex symbol and TV pitchman diminishes his accomplishments as one of the game's top right-handed hurlers. Palmer won 20 games in eight seasons, won 15 games a dozen times, and compiled sub-3.00 ERAs 10 times.

James Alvin Palmer (born in 1945) spent just one year in the minors before the Orioles promoted him in 1965. In 1966, he was inserted into the starting rotation and went 15-10 for the pennant-winning Birds. Jim gained fame that fall at age 20 by shutting out the Dodgers in Game 2 of the World Series, defeating Sandy Koufax.

Palmer missed most of the next two years with an arm injury, but came back in

1969 to win 16 games and pace the AL in winning percentage. In 1970, he began a streak of four consecutive 20-win seasons. In 1973, he won his first Cy Young Award with a 22-9 record and a league-best 2.40 ERA. After elbow problems in 1974, he rebounded to become one of the top hurlers in baseball. He led the AL in 1975 with a 2.09 ERA and 23 victories to cop his second Cy Young. He paced the AL in victories in 1976 (earning another Cy Young) and 1977. He won 20 games in 1978.

When Palmer notched his eighth 20-win season in 1978, only two other hurlers in AL history had as many: Walter Johnson (12) and Lefty Grove (eight).

Palmer allowed his share of home runs, but in 3,948 innings he never gave up a grand slam. Despite various injuries, he led the league in innings pitched four times. With Palmer on the staff, the Orioles won the American League West from 1969 to 1971, 1973, 1974, and 1979.

"That's like asking if I'd rather be hung or go to the electric chair."

—MERV RETTENMUND ON WHETHER HE'D RATHER FACE JIM PALMER OR TOM SEAVER

Jim and Oriole manager Earl Weaver were both highly competitive men. The two had many run-ins, but their relationship was not as rocky as many believed. Palmer retired in 1984 with a 2.86 career ERA, 268 wins, and 2,212 Ks. Over his 20-year career with the Orioles, Palmer compiled many club pitching records, and also picked up four Gold Gloves. He was named to the Hall of Fame in 1990.

				MAJOR LEAGUE TOTALS						
W	L	ERA	G	CG	IP	H	ER	BB	SO
268	152	2.86	558	211	3,948.0	3,349	1,252	1,311	2,212

EDDIE PLANK

PITCHER

PHILADELPHIA ATHLETICS 1901-1914
ST. LOUIS TERRIERS 1915
ST. LOUIS BROWNS 1916-1917

◆　　◆　　◆

BEFORE ENROLLING at Gettysburg College, Eddie Plank had no organized baseball experience. He was age 21 at the time and had spent his entire life on a farm. However, Gettysburg coach Frank Foreman, a former major-league pitcher, cajoled Plank into trying out for the varsity. From unlikely beginnings came a Hall of Fame career.

Although nearly 26 when he graduated in 1901, Edward Stewart Plank (1875-1926) was signed by the Philadelphia A's of the fledgling American League. Plank became a bane not only of enemy hitters, but also of umpires and sportswriters. His pitches were straightforward, but Plank worked so deliberately that he seemed to take forever between deliveries. Eddie claimed that he slowed the pace of the game to rattle hitters. Additionally, he kept them off-balance by talking to himself on the mound. His lack of overpowering stuff and the fact that he was so colorless as to be almost dull made him poor newspaper copy.

"[Plank's] motion was enough to give a batter nervous indigestion."

—EDDIE COLLINS

Plank won 20 or more games in a season seven times for the A's, a club record he shares with Lefty Grove. Plank never led the American League in wins, ERA, or strikeouts, nor was he ever considered the A's staff ace. He became one of the few Hall of Famers to ride the bench for an entire World Series when Mack instead used Jack Coombs and Chief Bender in the 1910 classic.

After slipping to 15 wins in 1914 and losing the second game of the World

Series that fall, Plank deserted the A's to play in the renegade Federal League. Thus, his 300th win came in the uniform of the 1915 St. Louis Terriers.

The 1904 Philadelphia A's were the only team in the century to boast two 25-game-winning left-handers: Plank and Rube Waddell.

The following year, the St. Louis Browns signed Plank. He finished his career in 1917 as the first southpaw in major-league history to win 300 games. Plank still holds the record for the most wins and the most shutouts by an AL left-hander.

MAJOR LEAGUE TOTALS									
W	L	ERA	G	CG	IP	H	ER	BB	SO
327	193	2.34	622	412	4,505.1	3,956	1,173	1,072	2,246

CAL RIPKEN

SHORTSTOP

BALTIMORE ORIOLES 1981-1996

❖　　　❖　　　❖

CAL RIPKEN HAD A JOB TO DO, and he did it every day. He broke Lou Gehrig's record for most consecutive games on September 6, 1995, playing in his 2,131st game.

While many modern players are derided for not putting enough effort into their jobs, Ripken never sat. His streak began in 1982, and he played 8,243 straight innings before sitting out the last two frames of a September 1987 blowout.

Drafted by the Orioles in 1978, Calvin Edwin Ripken Jr. (born in 1960) made his pro debut that year in the Appalachian League. He was an Oriole by late 1981.

In 1982, his first full big-league season, Ripken clubbed 29 home runs and chalked up 93 RBI to become the American League Rookie of the Year. After starting at third base, he shifted to shortstop in the middle of the campaign. At 6'4", Cal is the tallest full-time shortstop in major-league history.

In 1983, Ripken was the American League's Most Valuable Player and led Baltimore to a world championship. He hit .318 with 27 homers and paced the loop in hits and doubles. He also led in assists and double plays.

"The home run is sort of like a dunk in basketball. When you do it, everyone notices. And when you don't, everyone notices."

—CAL RIPKEN

The next year, Ripken batted .304 and again smacked 27 home runs. Ripken led the league in assists, putouts, double plays, fielding percentage, and chances per game at various points in his career, and collected two Gold Gloves. His brother, Billy, was the Orioles' regular second baseman for several years, and his father, Cal Sr., managed the team during the late 1980s.

On July 15, 1993, Ripken hit his 278th career home run as a shortstop, breaking Ernie Banks's record.

After several productive, but unspectacular, campaigns, Ripken exploded in 1991. He hit .323 with 34 homers and 114 RBI to win his second MVP Award and reestablish himself as one of the AL's top all-around players.

MAJOR LEAGUE TOTALS									
BA	G	AB	R	H	2B	3B	HR	RBI	SB
.277	2,381	9,217	1,366	2,549	487	43	353	1,369	35

ROBIN ROBERTS

P I T C H E R

PHILADELPHIA PHILLIES 1948-1961
BALTIMORE ORIOLES 1962-1965
HOUSTON ASTROS 1965-1966
CHICAGO CUBS 1966

◆   ◆   ◆

ROBIN ROBERTS WON 20 or more games each season from 1950 to 1955. He pitched in the majors for 19 years and won 286 games.

Robin Evan Roberts (born in 1926) was raised in Springfield, Illinois. He attended Michigan State University on a basketball scholarship in 1945 but eventually found his way to the diamond. He tossed two no-hitters at MSU and was signed by the Phillies in 1948.

The lanky right-hander joined the Phillies later in 1948 and went 7-9. Philadelphia finished sixth in '48, third in

'49, and won the NL title in 1950. In 1950, Roberts went 20-11 and was among the league leaders in nearly every significant category. That year was the first of six consecutive 20-plus win seasons for Roberts, but it was his only shot at a world championship.

"I can neither understand [his pinpoint control] nor explain it. I can't comprehend why other pitchers are wild."

—ROBIN ROBERTS

Roberts compiled a 28-7 mark in 1952, leading the league by a 10-win margin. He also paced the NL in victories from 1953 to 1955. Robin led the league in games started six straight years and complete games from 1952 to '56. He also won strikeout crowns in 1953 and 1954. He had outstanding control and extraordinary durability, leading the NL in innings four straight times while allowing very few walks. His great control also led to an all-time record of 505 home runs allowed, but the lack of enemy baserunners kept Roberts's ERAs low. Four times he held opposing hitters to the lowest on-base percentage in the league.

> ## "When Mickey Mantle bunted with the wind blowing out in Crosley Field."
>
> —ROBIN ROBERTS ON HIS GREATEST ALL-STAR GAME THRILL

The poor quality of his teams did not dim his ardor for baseball. His career ERA in 4,689 innings was 3.41. In addition to being a Hall of Fame pitcher, Roberts was also a key player in the development of the Players' Association.

MAJOR LEAGUE TOTALS									
W	L	ERA	G	CG	IP	H	ER	BB	SO
286	245	3.41	676	305	4,688.2	4,582	1,774	902	2,357

BROOKS ROBINSON

THIRD BASEMAN

BALTIMORE ORIOLES 1955-1977

❖   ❖   ❖

BROOKS ROBINSON revolutionized the third base position. He did with reflexes and intelligence what can't be accomplished with just quickness and a strong arm. He won 16 Gold Gloves and started 15 straight All-Star Games. Upon his retirement, Robinson held almost every major fielding record for third basemen, including games (2,870), fielding average (.971), putouts (2,697), assists (6,205), and double plays (618).

Born in Little Rock, Arkansas, in 1937, Brooks Calbert Robinson was signed by Baltimore in 1955, and by 1960 was the regular Oriole third baseman. For the next four years, he was a respectable offensive and defensive performer.

In 1964, Robinson's .317 average, career-high 28 homers, league-leading 118 RBI, and sterling glove work earned him AL MVP honors even though the Orioles finished third. Frank Robinson joined Baltimore in 1966, and the Birds won their first World Series. Brooks contributed a .269 average, 23 homers, and 100 RBI.

"Brooks is not a fast man, but his arms and legs move very quickly."
—CURT GOWDY

Robinson's work in the 1970 World Series earned him Most Valuable Player honors; he hit .429 with two home runs and a highlight reel full of defensive gems. "The Human Vacuum Cleaner" dominated the World Series as perhaps no other defender ever has.

In 23 seasons, Brooks had over 20 homers six times and cleared 80 RBI eight times. He collected 2,848 hits, 268 home runs, and 1,357 RBI. Robinson led AL third basemen in assists eight times, fielding average 11 times, putouts and double plays three times, and total chances per game twice.

> *"I walked back to the dugout appreciating his play for what it was—a thing of beauty."*
> —JOHNNY BENCH AFTER BEING ROBBED OF A HIT BY ROBINSON IN THE 1970 WORLD SERIES

After retiring in 1977, he became a popular broadcaster in Baltimore. Robinson's 1983 induction into the Hall of Fame drew one of the largest crowds ever seen at Cooperstown.

				MAJOR LEAGUE TOTALS					
BA	G	AB	R	H	2B	3B	HR	RBI	SB
.267	2,896	10,654	1,232	2,848	482	68	268	1,357	28

FRANK ROBINSON

O U T F I E L D E R

CINCINNATI REDS 1956-1965
BALTIMORE ORIOLES 1966-1971
LOS ANGELES DODGERS 1972
CALIFORNIA ANGELS 1973-1974
CLEVELAND INDIANS 1974-1976

◆   ◆   ◆

FRANK ROBINSON was the first player to win Most Valuable Player Awards in both leagues and the first African-American manager in the majors.

Born in 1935, Robinson signed with Cincinnati in 1953. He led the Sally League in 1954 with 112 runs scored, batting .336 with 25 homers and 110 RBI.

Robinson joined the Reds in 1956 and won the Rookie of the Year Award, leading the league with 122 runs and hitting .290 with 38 homers. His excellent production from 1957 to '60 made him one of the top outfielders in the National League. Robby was also a fine defensive player with good speed, and won a Gold Glove in 1958.

"If I had one wish in the world today, it would be that Jackie Robinson could be here to see this happen."

—FRANK ROBINSON ON BEING NAMED THE FIRST BLACK MANAGER, IN THE FALL OF 1974

Frank's 1961 MVP performance led the Reds to a pennant. He paced the loop with a .611 slugging percentage and batted .323 with 37 homers, 117 runs scored, 124 RBI, and 22 stolen bases. The next year, he led the NL in slugging percentage for the third consecutive time.

In December 1965, he was dealt to Baltimore. Cincinnati GM Bill DeWitt said, "Robinson is not a young 30." All the supposedly finished Robinson did in 1966 was win the Triple Crown and MVP Award, hitting .316 with 49 homers. He also smacked two home runs as the O's won the World Series. The Orioles won AL pennants from 1969 to '71; Robinson hit 85 homers in that span.

"Close don't count in baseball. Close only counts in horseshoes and hand grenades."

—FRANK ROBINSON

In 1974, Robinson went to Cleveland, and the next year was named the Indians' player-manager. Only Babe Ruth, Willie Mays, and Hank Aaron socked more home runs than Frank's 586. In 1982, the Hall of Fame opened its doors to Robinson.

MAJOR LEAGUE TOTALS									
BA	G	AB	R	H	2B	3B	HR	RBI	SB
.294	2,808	10,006	1,829	2,943	528	72	586	1,812	204

JACKIE ROBINSON

BROOKLYN DODGERS 1947-1956

◆　　　◆　　　◆

DURING THE FIRST HALF of this century, a color line excluding African Americans extended to nearly every field of endeavor. There was a great inertia that needed to be overcome in order to create the integrated society promised in the Constitution. That first high-profile integration came on a baseball diamond, and the first black man to cross the white lines was Jackie Robinson.

Jack Roosevelt Robinson (1919-1972) grew up in Pasadena, California, in a poor neighborhood. His brother, Mack, participated in the 1936 Summer Olympics in Berlin. Jackie, too, was an outstanding athlete; he went to UCLA and starred in four sports. He broke the Pacific Coast Conference record in the broad jump and twice was the PCC's leading scorer in basketball. He led the nation in yards per carry in football and was a baseball star. In 1941, he played with the Los Angeles Bulldogs pro football team. After the Pearl Harbor attack, Jackie attended Officer Candidate School in Kansas, making it to second lieutenant. In 1944, he was threatened with a court martial because he refused to sit in the back of an Army bus; he instead received an honorable discharge.

Robinson joined the Kansas City Monarchs of the Negro League after his discharge. It wasn't long before Dodgers general manager Branch Rickey chose Robinson to be the first African American in the major leagues. Jackie was chosen for many reasons. Aside from being an outstanding athlete and baseball player, he had many character strengths. Rickey impressed upon Jackie the need to turn the other cheek. From the beginning, Jackie was everything Rickey wanted.

Robinson first broke the color line with Montreal of the International League in 1946 and led the league with a .349 batting average. With the Dodgers in 1947, Robinson was Rookie of the Year. He said that his lowest day his rookie year was his first visit to Philadelphia, when he could "scarcely believe my ears. Almost as if it had been synchronized by some master conductor, hate poured forth from the Phillies dugout." Jackie said he was never closer to quitting.

"To do what [Robinson] did has got to be the most tremendous thing I've ever seen in sports."

—PEE WEE REESE

Jackie was also combative after the most overt racism had faded. He refused to be someone he was not, refused to conform to an image of a man who "knew his place." It is important to his memory that he not only took the first step to integrate the majors, but he took the next step, too.

He was not afraid to let his talent speak for itself and to be himself.

Jackie won a batting title in 1949 at .342 on the way to being named the league's Most Valuable Player. Though he played just 10 seasons, he helped the Dodgers to six World Series, winning one; the Dodgers were often the victims of the Yankee buzz saw.

Robinson was the most devastating baserunner of his day and a fine basestealer. He had dangerous home run power and was exceptionally difficult to strike out, fanning only 291 times. He played his first season for the Dodgers at first base, an unfamiliar position, and set a record for rookie double plays that still stands. Later he became one of the very best second basemen in history. Robinson retired in 1957 and was inducted into the Hall of Fame in 1962.

MAJOR LEAGUE TOTALS									
BA	G	AB	R	H	2B	3B	HR	RBI	SB
.311	1,382	4,877	947	1,518	273	54	137	734	197

PETE ROSE

S E C O N D   B A S E M A N
T H I R D   B A S E M A N
O U T F I E L D E R
F I R S T   B A S E M A N

CINCINNATI REDS 1963-1978; 1984-1986
PHILADELPHIA PHILLIES 1979-1983
MONTREAL EXPOS 1984

◆   ◆   ◆

PETE ROSE IS BASEBALL'S all-time leader with 4,256 career hits. In 1985, he broke Ty Cobb's seemingly unbreakable career hit record. Still, Rose is not in the Hall of Fame.

Rose, like Cobb, squeezed every bit of production from his talent. Both men seemed slightly out of place off the diamond, and both had gambling troubles at the end of their careers. Cobb was exonerated, but, acting on evidence that suggested Rose had bet on baseball games while managing the Reds, Commissioner Bart Giamatti banned Rose from baseball for life in 1989.

The Reds signed 140-pound Cincinnatian Peter Edward Rose (born in 1941) in 1960. He spent the off-season pumping iron, and led in runs, hits, and triples his next two years in the minors.

"The only way I can't hit .300 is if there is something physically wrong with me."

—PETE ROSE

Rose debuted in 1963 as Cincy's second sacker, and his enthusiasm endeared him to hometown fans. Taking a walk, he dashed to first emulating Enos Slaughter; Whitey Ford dubbed Rose "Charley Hustle." Rose's .273 batting average and 101 runs scored won him the Rookie of the Year Award.

Rose came back in 1965 to lead the NL in hits and putouts by a second baseman. He was named to his first of 17 All-Star teams. In 1967, the Reds moved Rose to the outfield, and in 1968 and '69, he captured batting titles.

Rose led the "Big Red Machine" to four World Series between 1970 and '76. In 1973, he batted .338 and won the NL MVP Award. He amassed a 44-game hitting streak in 1977 and collected hit No. 3,000 the next year.

"With all the money I'm making, I should be playing two positions."

—PETE ROSE AFTER SIGNING WITH THE PHILLIES

Rose signed with Philadelphia and played on the 1980 world championship squad. He finished his career as a player-manager with the Reds in 1986, compiling a .303 lifetime average. His 3,562 games and 14,053 at bats are major-league records, and he ranks second in career doubles.

MAJOR LEAGUE TOTALS									
BA	G	AB	R	H	2B	3B	HR	RBI	SB
.303	3,562	14,053	2,165	4,256	746	125	160	1,314	198

AMOS RUSIE

P I T C H E R

INDIANAPOLIS HOOSIERS 1889
NEW YORK GIANTS 1890-1895, 1897-1898
CINCINNATI REDS 1901

◆　　　◆　　　◆

AMOS RUSIE is one of the few players in the Hall of Fame who spent fewer than 10 seasons in the major leagues. Despite losing over two years due to disputes with his employers, Rusie won 243 games and paced the NL in strikeouts five times.

Born in Mooresville, Indiana, Amos Wilson Rusie (1871-1942) was signed at age 18 by the Indianapolis Hoosiers (then in the National League), who valued the local boy for his drawing card appeal and blinding velocity.

By 1890, Rusie had joined the New York Giants and led all National League hurlers with 341 strikeouts. Gotham was not an ideal milieu for the young fireballer, however, who soon developed a drinking problem to go along with his control problems on the mound. Worse, he could not escape miserly Giants owner Andrew Freedman, one of the most repressive owners in major-league history.

In the pitcher's box, though, "The Hoosier Thunderbolt" was in his element. Rusie's blazing speed helped convince the game's rulemakers to move the pitching mound from 50' from home plate to 60'6".

Rusie won his 243rd and final major-league game in 1898 when he was just 27 years old.

Although Rusie's strikeouts dipped sharply in 1893, the first year the mound was situated at its present location, he still led the league by a total nearly double that of runner-up Brickyard Kennedy. After topping the loop in whiffs again the next two seasons, Rusie sat out all 1896 when Freedman first attempted to fine him $200 and then cut his pay. Returning in 1897, when the other clubs kicked in $5,000 to reimburse him for the salary he had lost in 1896, Rusie had two more strong years with the Giants. Wounded by Freedman's skinflint methods again, Amos skipped the 1899 season, then was prevented by personal problems from playing in 1900.

Reds owner John Brush was about to purchase part of the Giants in 1901. So before the 1901 campaign, Rusie was traded to Cincinnati for Christy Mathewson in a one-sided deal. While Mathewson went on to win 372 games in the majors, Rusie proved to be all washed up. Rusie was, however, named to the Hall of Fame in 1977.

MAJOR LEAGUE TOTALS									
W	L	ERA	G	CG	IP	H	ER	BB	SO
243	160	3.07	462	392	3,769.2	3,384	1,286	1,716	1,957

BABE RUTH

PITCHER
OUTFIELDER

BOSTON RED SOX 1914-1919
NEW YORK YANKEES 1920-1934
BOSTON BRAVES 1935

◆　　　◆　　　◆

IN 1914, WHEN BABE RUTH was age 20, he was 6'2" and a slim 180 pounds of muscle—and a superb left-handed pitcher. His prowess with the bat, however, prompted his manager to cut in half the number of starts of this young ace in 1918 and give him 317 at bats playing as a regular outfielder. He went 13-7 pitching and led the league with 11 home runs. The kid became the talk of both leagues. The finest player in the history of the game was just beginning to flex his muscles, but everyone already knew about Ruth.

In 1919, George Herman Ruth (1895-1948) set a single-season record with 29 home runs and led the league in RBI and runs for the Boston Red Sox. Red Sox owner Harry Frazee's financial needs prompted Ruth's sale to the New York Yankees. "The Sultan of Swat" brought $100,000, more than twice the price of any previous player, and a $300,000 loan.

"I have only one superstition. I make sure to touch all the bases when I hit a home run."

—BABE RUTH

In 1920, Ruth took New York, baseball, and America by storm. His 54 home runs were more than any other AL team total. His .847 slugging average still stands as the single-season record, and he hit .322 with a league-leading 158 runs and 137 RBI. He dominated the AL almost up to his 1935 retirement: a batting title in 1924, 12 home run titles, eight times leading the league in runs, six in RBI, and 13 times in slugging. He might have won more honors, but in 1922 he was suspended by the commissioner for barnstorming, and he played in only 110 games. He was limited to only 98 games in 1925, when he was sidelined with an intestinal abscess; "Babe's Bellyache" was front-page news across the country. Despite his big swing, the Bambino led the league in walks 11 times, including a record 170 in 1923. He still holds lifetime marks in walks and slugging. He led the way for a new, high-offense baseball that packed in fans in record numbers.

The Babe led the Yankees to seven World Series appearances and four championships. He teamed with Lou Gehrig to form the most feared one-two punch in baseball history, and in 1927 the fabled "Murderer's Row" of the Yankees won 110 games and lost just 44. Ruth set a record that year that was to capture the imagination like no other, hitting 60 home runs in a single season. He further added to baseball lore in the 1932 World Series, when, as legend has it, he made his famous "Called Shot." He reportedly pointed to the center field bleachers before homering against the Cubs.

> *"[Ruth's] stomach used to rumble in the outfield if the other team had a big inning."*
>
> —JIM MURRAY

Beyond his on-field heroics, Ruth—one of the first five players inducted into the Hall of Fame in 1936—was a legend for his off-the-field adventures as well. He was genial and absent-minded, with an appetite for life that led him to every excess. He made friends everywhere—while he ate everything, drank everything, tried everything. He was the most beloved player ever to play the game. The Hall of Fame was created for players like Babe Ruth. He died in 1948 of throat cancer.

			MAJOR LEAGUE TOTALS						
BA	G	AB	R	H	2B	3B	HR	RBI	SB
.342	2,503	8,399	2,174	2,873	506	136	714	2,211	123

NOLAN RYAN

PITCHER

NEW YORK METS 1966-1971
CALIFORNIA ANGELS 1972-1979
HOUSTON ASTROS 1980-1988
TEXAS RANGERS 1989-1993

◆   ◆   ◆

THE SINGLE-SEASON and all-time strikeout leader, Nolan Ryan was one of the hardest throwers in baseball history. He used his fastball to garner seven no-hitters and 324 wins over his 27-year career.

The New York Mets drafted Lynn Nolan Ryan (born in 1947) in 1965. He reached the majors permanently in 1968 and was a key member of the 1969 "Miracle Mets," setting an NLCS record for most strikeouts by a reliever.

Ryan was traded to the Angels in 1971 for Jim Fregosi. In 1972, he was 19-16 with a league-leading 329 Ks. In 1973, he threw two no-hitters, set a single-season record with 383 strikeouts, and collected his first 20-win season. His heater picked up the "Ryan Express" appellation in reference to the film *Von Ryan's Express*. During his eight seasons with California, he led the American League in strikeouts seven times (and in walks on six occasions).

In 1974, Ryan set an AL record for most wins by a last-place ballclub, winning 22 games for the California Angels.

In 1980, Ryan signed a free-agent deal with the Houston Astros to be close to his Texas home. Nolan thrived at the Astrodome, pacing the National League with a 1.69 ERA in 1981. He also led the loop in ERA and strikeouts in 1987 but finished just 8-16 due to poor support. In the 1980s, he improved his control significantly, going from a high of 204 walks in 1977 to totals under 100 over his last 10 years. He signed with Texas in 1989 and pitched for the Rangers for the remaining five seasons of his career.

"If Ryan would act his age, there might be a few records left for me."
—ROGER CLEMENS

Ryan, the only pitcher with three straight seasons of 300 or more strikeouts, is also the sole major-league hurler with more than four no-hitters. He tossed his fifth on national television in the heat of the 1981 pennant race. His seventh gem came in 1991 against the Toronto Blue Jays, when Ryan was 44 years old. He won 11 strikeout crowns, finished with a total of 5,174 Ks, and threw bullets until the day he retired in 1993.

					MAJOR LEAGUE TOTALS					
W	L	ERA	G	CG	IP	H	ER	BB	SO
324	292	3.19	807	222	5,386.0	3,923	1,911	2,795	5,714

RYNE
SANDBERG

S E C O N D   B A S E M A N

PHILADELPHIA PHILLIES 1981
CHICAGO CUBS 1982-1994; 1996

◆   ◆   ◆

PHILLIES PRESIDENT BILL GILES was so eager to trade Larry Bowa to the Cubs for Ivan DeJesus in 1981 that he threw in Ryne Sandberg, who went on to become baseball's best second baseman of the 1980s and the early '90s.

Ryne Dee Sandberg, born in 1959 in Spokane, Washington, starred in three sports in high school and was drafted by the Phillies in 1978. In his Cub debut in 1982, Sandberg played 140 games at third base. He hit .271 and scored 103 runs. Moved to second base the last month of the season, he quickly adapted to his new position. In 1983, Sandberg became the first National League player ever to win a

Gold Glove in his first season at a new position.

Sandberg led Chicago into their first NLCS appearance in 1984 by clubbing 19 home runs, batting .314, winning another Gold Glove, and leading the league with 114 runs and 19 triples. For his efforts, he was named the National League's Most Valuable Player.

In 1989 and 1990, Sandberg set a record for second basemen with 123 straight errorless games.

The next year, Sandberg became the third player ever with 25 home runs and 50 stolen bases in a season. Sandberg's 54 swipes were the most by a Cub since Frank Chance's 57 in 1906.

Sandberg broke a National League record in 1986 by making just five errors all season. In 1989, his 30 home runs led the Cubs to another NL East title. In 1990, Sandberg powered a loop-best 40 homers. Ryne was the first second baseman since Rogers Hornsby in 1925 to lead the league in homers.

When he began 1994 batting .238 through 57 games for a struggling club, the future Hall of Famer decided to retire at age 34. "I am not the type of person who can be satisfied with anything less than my very best effort," he said. However, after a year-and-a-half absence, Ryno grew itchy for the game he loved and announced he would return to the Cubs in '96. That year, he slugged 25 homers and had 92 RBI.

MAJOR LEAGUE TOTALS									
BA	G	AB	R	H	2B	3B	HR	RBI	SB
.286	2,029	7,938	1,264	2,268	377	76	270	997	337

RON SANTO

THIRD BASEMAN

CHICAGO CUBS 1960-1973
CHICAGO WHITE SOX 1974

◆　　　◆　　　◆

RON SANTO MAY BE BEST remembered as the leader of the ill-fated 1969 Cubs squad, but from 1960 to 1973, he was the top all-around third baseman in the National League.

The Cubs brought Ronald Edward Santo (born in 1940) to the majors in 1960 after less than two full seasons of pro ball. In 1961, his first full big-league season, he batted .284 with 23 home runs and 83 RBI.

Santo came into his own in 1963, batting .297 with 25 homers and 99 RBI. In 1964, he hit 30 more dingers with 96 RBI and a career-best .313 average. Meanwhile, Santo drove in over 100 runs four times, including a high of 123 in 1969. A very patient hitter, Ron led the league four times in walks and hit over .300 three times. He was a nine-time All-Star.

"Funny, but there is less pressure being three or four games behind in a pennant race than three or four ahead. Last year, we kept looking back over our shoulder."

—RON SANTO IN 1970

Santo was a victim of the Cubs' youth movement after the 1973 season despite his 20 home runs. Chicago dealt him to the Angels, but Santo invoked the "five-and-10" clause that allowed players with 10 years experience, and five on one club, to deny a trade. He wanted to stay in Chicago, so he was instead sent to the White Sox. However, the Sox used Santo at second base, then first base, and finally at designated hitter in 1974. The switching hindered Santo, who hit just .221 before retiring after his south side season with 2,254 career hits.

Santo was also the best defensive third baseman in the NL during the 1960s, and he won Gold Gloves every year from 1964 to 1968.

Unbeknownst to most fans during his playing career, Santo suffered from diabetes. He has been a spokesman in the fight against the disease, and became a radio announcer for the Cubs after his playing career.

MAJOR LEAGUE TOTALS									
BA	G	AB	R	H	2B	3B	HR	RBI	SB
.277	2,243	8,143	1,138	2,254	365	67	342	1,331	35

MIKE SCHMIDT

THIRD BASEMAN
FIRST BASEMAN

PHILADELPHIA PHILLIES 1973-1989

◆　　　◆　　　◆

YOUNG MIKE SCHMIDT was Philadelphia's starting third baseman in 1973. He hit 18 homers but batted a paltry .196 and fanned 136 times in only 367 at bats. From that beginning, Schmidt went on to become one of the best third basemen in baseball history.

Michael Jack Schmidt (born in 1949) was a college All-American at Ohio University and was drafted by the Phillies in 1971. Schmidt prospered in Eugene in 1972, posting a .291 average with 26 home runs and 91 RBI.

After his dismal 1973 season, Schmidt could have easily lost his job, but the Phillies' faith in him paid off the next year. He won his first of eight National League home run crowns with 36 blasts, drove in

116 runs, and pumped his average to .282. He also won homer crowns in 1975 and '76 with 38 dingers each year. Schmidt was a 12-time All-Star, and helped the Phillies win six NL East titles.

In 1984, Schmidt became the first major-leaguer to end up in a tie for both his loop's home run and RBI crowns in the same season.

Schmidt's best season came in 1980, when his league-leading 48 dingers and 121 RBI led the Phillies to their first world championship. In the Series, he batted .381 with three homers and seven RBI. Mike was named both the National League Most Valuable Player and the World Series MVP that year.

Only Hank Aaron and Willie Mays had hit more National League round-trippers than Schmidt's 548 when Mike retired. He topped 30 homers 13 times and surpassed the 35-homer barrier 11 times. Only Babe

Ruth's nine league home run titles top Schmidt's eight crowns.

"Philadelphia is the only city where you can experience the thrill of victory and the agony of reading about it the next day."

—MIKE SCHMIDT

Schmidt was the best defensive third baseman in the league for many seasons, winning 10 Gold Gloves. He also broke numerous NL fielding records. He retired in 1989 after playing his entire career with the Phillies.

MAJOR LEAGUE TOTALS									
BA	G	AB	R	H	2B	3B	HR	RBI	SB
.267	2,404	8,352	1,506	2,234	408	59	548	1,595	174

TOM SEAVER

PITCHER

New York Mets 1967-1977; 1983
Cincinnati Reds 1977-1982
Chicago White Sox 1984-1986
Boston Red Sox 1986

◆　　　◆　　　◆

TOM SEAVER'S 25 WINS carried the New York Mets to a stunning pennant in 1969 and earned him the nickname "Tom Terrific." In his 20-year career, Seaver set a multitude of Met and National League pitching records and captured three Cy Young Awards.

Unlike most pitching greats, George Thomas Seaver (born in 1944) did not attract the notice of major-league scouts until he was in college. The Atlanta Braves offered him a $40,000 bonus in 1966 to sign. The contract was voided, however, by Commissioner William Eckert, who held a lottery for any team who agreed to match or top the Braves' offer. The Mets stepped in, picked the lucky number, and signed Seaver.

In 1969, 1973, and 1975, Seaver won Cy Young Awards, and twice he hurled the Mets to a pennant. The team's second flag came in 1973 when Seaver won 19 games and paced the NL in ERA and strikeouts. In all, Seaver paced the senior circuit five times in whiffs and fanned over 200 men a season a record nine straight campaigns. His 3,640 punchouts are fourth on the all-time list.

"They called us 'The Miracle Mets.' Miracle, my eye. What happened was that a lot of good young players suddenly jelled and matured all at once."
—TOM SEAVER

In 1977, Seaver was traded to Cincinnati, where he had seasons of 14-3 and 14-2. After six years in Cincy, the Mets reacquired him before the 1983 season. After a 9-14 campaign, however, he was drafted by the Chicago White Sox.

Seaver won 31 games in his first two seasons in Chicago and nailed down his 300th career victory in 1985. When he began poorly in 1986, he was dealt to Boston. He retired after the season with a .603 career winning percentage, the highest of any 300-game winner in the past half-century. Seaver was overwhelmingly named to the Hall of Fame in 1992.

MAJOR LEAGUE TOTALS									
W	L	ERA	G	CG	IP	H	ER	BB	SO
311	205	2.86	656	231	4,782.2	3,971	1,521	1,390	3,640

AL SIMMONS

OUTFIELDER

PHILADELPHIA ATHLETICS 1924-1932;
1940-1941; 1944
CHICAGO WHITE SOX 1933-1935
DETROIT TIGERS 1936
WASHINGTON SENATORS 1937-1938
BOSTON BRAVES 1939
CINCINNATI REDS 1939
BOSTON RED SOX 1943

◆　　　◆　　　◆

AL SIMMONS'S career .334 average mocked those who criticized his peculiar penchant for striding toward third base when he swung. The unorthodox batting style of this right-handed hitter led to the tag "Bucketfoot Al," but Simmons had the last laugh when he reached the Hall of Fame.

Aloys Szymanski (1902-1956) never wanted to be anything but a baseball player. In 1922, he signed his first contract with the Milwaukee Brewers of the American Association. When Al hit .398 in 24 games in 1923, the Philadelphia Athletics bought him for around $50,000.

In 1924, his rookie year, Simmons batted .308 and knocked home 102 runs. The following year, he collected a league-leading 253 hits, hiked his average to .387, and became the first player in American League history to drive in 100 or more runs in each of his first two seasons in the majors.

"If only I could have nine players named Simmons."

—CONNIE MACK

Simmons hit 307 lifetime home runs and was also a good outfielder with a strong arm. When Ty Cobb joined the A's in 1927, he helped Al to develop even further. Simmons, in fact, found it easy to befriend the much-shunned Cobb. Paradoxically, in his dedication to becoming the best player possible, Simmons himself acquired a reputation for not being personable.

The A's took three straight pennants starting in 1929, and Al enjoyed the first of five straight seasons of 200 or more hits. The following year he won his first of two consecutive batting crowns and was generally regarded as the AL's best player.

Simmons was the first player in American League history to drive in 100 or more runs in each of his first two seasons in the majors.

Simmons was traded to the Chicago White Sox in 1933 for economic reasons. Later Al played for Detroit, Washington, and Boston before spending one season in the NL. He returned to the A's in 1944 to finish his career. A coach for the A's during the 1940s, Simmons acted as unofficial manager when Connie Mack grew too old to serve capably.

MAJOR LEAGUE TOTALS									
BA	G	AB	R	H	2B	3B	HR	RBI	SB
.334	2,215	8,761	1,507	2,927	539	149	307	1,827	87

GEORGE SISLER

St. Louis Browns 1915-1927
Washington Senators 1928
Boston Braves 1928-1930

◆   ◆   ◆

GEORGE SISLER was one of the best first basemen who ever played the game. Injuries allowed him to play at peak capacity for only half of his career. With luck, however, he might have been the greatest hitter of them all.

George Harold Sisler (1893-1973) of Akron, Ohio, signed a pro contract while still in high school. He later enrolled at the University of Michigan to play under the legendary Branch Rickey. His contract was bought by Pittsburgh, but George also signed with Rickey's St. Louis Browns. The National Commission ruled in favor of the Browns.

Sisler began his career as a pitcher. After joining the Browns, in fact, he out-dueled Walter Johnson. Playing first base in 1916, Sisler hit .305 in his first full season. After three successive years of batting around .350, George went wild in 1920. Not only did he top the American League with a .407 average, but he collected an all-time record 257 hits and clouted 19 home runs. Sisler almost never struck out, led the AL four times in stolen bases, and played fine defense.

Sisler broke into the big leagues in 1915 as a pitcher, notching a pair of complete-game victories over Walter Johnson.

In 1922, Sisler raised the ante by batting .420. He also paced the AL in runs, steals, hits, and triples, and won the league's MVP Award. Even with all of Sisler's heroics, the Browns still finished second to the Yankees by a single game.

Unfortunately, George began to develop double vision, stemming from his infected sinuses. He missed all of 1923, and an operation only partially remedied the problem. When Sisler returned in 1924, he slumped to .305. He never felt he was quite the same player and closed his major-league career with the Senators and the Boston Braves.

Sisler ended his career in 1928. Father of three sons who played pro ball, he joined the Hall of Fame in 1939.

MAJOR LEAGUE TOTALS									
BA	G	AB	R	H	2B	3B	HR	RBI	SB
.340	2,055	8,267	1,284	2,812	425	165	100	1,175	375

OZZIE SMITH

S H O R T S T O P

SAN DIEGO PADRES 1978-1981
ST. LOUIS CARDINALS 1982-1996

◆　　　◆　　　◆

J UST LIKE THE MYTHICAL Wizard of Oz, Ozzie Smith made everything look easy. He fielded almost flawlessly at shortstop, hit better than most shortstops, and stole bases with ease.

Osborne Earl Smith (born in 1954) did not sign a pro contract until age 22 because he wanted to finish college. The San Diego Padres drafted him in 1977.

Smith started 1978 as San Diego's shortstop, notching 40 stolen bases and pacing the National League with 28 sacrifice hits. For his efforts, he finished second in Rookie of the Year balloting. He also registered 548 assists, the first of a record eight times he tallied 500 or more assists. A defining play in Smith's career came that April. Ozzie dove to his left for a Jeff Burroughs roller and, as the ball unexpectedly bounced up, he amazingly grabbed it bare-handed and threw Burroughs out.

In 1979, Smith led the National League shortstops with 555 assists, and won his first of an amazing 13 straight Gold Gloves the next year. Smith also stole 57 bases in 1980.

Smith in 1980 set a major-league record for most assists by a shortstop, with 621. The old mark was 601 assists by Glenn Wright in 1924.

On February 11, 1982, Smith was traded to the Cardinals for star shortstop Garry Templeton. Some felt the Padres won the trade (Templeton was a better hitter), but the reverse turned out to be true. Smith became an even more valuable defender in Busch Stadium than he had been in San Diego, and he chipped in offensively. The Cards won the World Series the year Ozzie joined the team.

Smith developed line-drive power, began drawing more walks, and hit .270 or over almost every year. In 1985, he hit .276 with six homers. His home run won Game 5 of the NLCS. Smith's best season was 1987, when his .303 average, 182 hits, 104 runs scored, and 75 RBI led to a second-place MVP finish. Ozzie really did get better with age, and he carved out a position for himself among the all-time great shortstops.

	MAJOR LEAGUE TOTALS								
BA	G	AB	R	H	2B	3B	HR	RBI	SB
.262	2,573	9,396	1,257	2,460	402	69	28	793	580

DUKE SNIDER

O U T F I E L D E R

BROOKLYN DODGERS 1947-1957
LOS ANGELES DODGERS 1958-1962
NEW YORK METS 1963
SAN FRANCISCO GIANTS 1964

◆　　　◆　　　◆

AN UNPRECEDENTED concentration of talent played center field in New York in the 1950s. The Yankees had Mickey Mantle, the Giants had Willie Mays, and Duke Snider played for Brooklyn. From 1954 to 1957, Snider had the most home runs and RBI of the three, and he totaled more homers and RBI than any player of the 1950s.

Born in 1926 in Compton, California, Edwin Donald Snider signed with the Dodgers in 1944. He played his first game for the Dodgers the same day that Jackie Robinson did, in 1947. However, Snider, a good minor-league hitter, hit just .241 with 24 strikeouts in 83 at bats before being demoted to St. Paul. Snider spent most of 1948 in Montreal, where Branch Rickey put Duke through a strict regimen to teach him the strike zone. Snider learned enough to walk 80 or more times four straight seasons.

"My high salary for one season was $46,000 and a Cadillac. If I were to get paid a million, I'd feel that I should sweep out the stadium every night after I finished playing the game."

—DUKE SNIDER

Soon, Snider delivered left-handed power for the Boys of Summer. He hit .292 with 23 homers in 1949, and in 1950 hit 31 round-trippers while pacing the NL in hits. He led the league in runs scored each year from 1953 to '55. Snider, Babe Ruth, and Ralph Kiner are the only men in baseball history to hit at least 40 homers five straight times.

The Duke, a regular on six Dodger pennant winners, hit four homers twice in World Series competition and ranks fourth with 11 home runs in Series play. Snider also totaled an impressive .594 slugging percentage in World Series competition. In addition to belting 407 lifetime home runs, Snider also played outstanding defense and had a great throwing arm.

Knee and elbow injuries reduced Duke to part-time play beginning in 1960. He spent a year with the Mets in 1963, enjoying playing in New York (but not with the Mets), and retired after a year with the Giants in 1964. A broadcaster for the Expos in the 1970s, Snider joined the Hall of Fame in 1980.

MAJOR LEAGUE TOTALS									
BA	G	AB	R	H	2B	3B	HR	RBI	SB
.295	2,143	7,161	1,259	2,116	358	85	407	1,333	99

WARREN SPAHN

PITCHER

BOSTON BRAVES 1942; 1946-1952
MILWAUKEE BRAVES 1953-1964
NEW YORK METS 1965
SAN FRANCISCO GIANTS 1965

◆　　　◆　　　◆

WARREN SPAHN'S 363 career wins are still more than any other left-hander in history. Despite not winning his first big-league game until age 25, he anchored Braves' staffs for almost 20 years. Spahn led the National League in wins a record eight times, complete games a record nine times, and strikeouts four years in a row.

Born in Buffalo in 1921, Warren Edward Spahn was the son of an avid amateur baseball player. Warren grew up as a first baseman, but soon switched to pitching. Signed by the Braves in 1940, he led the Three-I League in 1941 with 19 wins and a 1.83 ERA. Spahn was off to war for the next three years, where he earned a Bronze Star and a Purple Heart.

Warren returned in 1946 and went 8-5. He bloomed in 1947, winning 21 and leading the NL with a 2.33 ERA. In 1948, he teamed with Johnny Sain in the famous "Spahn and Sain and pray for rain" rotation. Sain won 24, Warren took 15, and the Braves won the pennant before bowing to Cleveland in the World Series.

"A pitcher needs two pitches—one they're looking for and one to cross 'em up."

—WARREN SPAHN

In 1949, Spahn led the NL in victories, complete games, innings, and strikeouts. He paced the loop with 21 wins and 191 Ks in 1950. Spahn then captured 22 in 1951, a league-best 23 in 1953, 21 in 1954, and 20 in 1956. After losing velocity on his fastball, he simply developed new pitches and depended on his vast knowledge of NL hitters.

Spahn went 21-11 in 1957 and 22-11 in 1958 as the Braves captured two pennants and a World Series. The seemingly ageless hurler cleared 20 wins from 1959 to '61 and again in 1963 before retiring in 1965. Warren still ranks in the top 10 for career wins, innings pitched, and shutouts, and his 13 20-win seasons are unsurpassed.

MAJOR LEAGUE TOTALS									
W	L	ERA	G	CG	IP	H	ER	BB	SO
363	245	3.09	750	382	5,243.2	4,830	1,798	1,434	2,583

TRIS SPEAKER

O U T F I E L D E R

BOSTON RED SOX 1907-1915
CLEVELAND INDIANS 1916-1926
WASHINGTON SENATORS 1927
PHILADELPHIA ATHLETICS 1928

◆　　　　◆　　　　◆

THE EVIDENCE SHOWS THAT Tris Speaker was the best defensive center fielder of his era, if not ever. He revolutionized outfield play more than any other player in history. In addition, Speaker was also a tremendous batsman who collected 3,514 career hits.

Born in Hubbard, Texas, Tristram E. Speaker (1888-1958) started in baseball as a pitcher. When converted to the outfield, Speaker played such a shallow center field that he was, in effect, a fifth infielder. In the dead-ball era, when long drives were rare, other outfielders copied Speaker to cut down on bloop hits. In the lively ball era of the early 1920s, Speaker was the only center fielder who could continue to play shallow and still chase down long hits. He possessed great speed, unparalleled instincts, and a strong throwing arm.

"It would be useless for any player to attempt to explain successful batting."

—Tris Speaker

Tris joined the Red Sox in 1908. In 1912, Speaker played on his first of two world championship teams in the Hub while pacing the American League in doubles, home runs, and on-base percentage. During his career, "The Grey Eagle" topped the junior circuit in two-base hits a record eight times. His 792 doubles are still more than any other player in history. He batted over .300 18 times, and his .344 average is fifth on the all-time list.

A salary dispute resulted in a trade to Cleveland after the 1915 season. In 1916, Tris hit .386 to win the batting crown. In

July 1919, the Indians named Speaker player-manager. The next year, Cleveland gained its first pennant as Tris batted .388.

In 1920, Speaker set a major-league record with 11 consecutive base hits.

In 1926, when implicated in a game-fixing scandal involving Ty Cobb, Speaker quit the Indians. He and Cobb were exonerated, though, when their accuser, former pitcher Dutch Leonard, refused to confront the pair in person. Speaker returned to play two more seasons, and was enshrined in the Hall of Fame in 1937.

MAJOR LEAGUE TOTALS

BA	G	AB	R	H	2B	3B	HR	RBI	SB
.344	2,789	10,208	1,881	3,515	792	223	117	1,559	433

WILLIE STARGELL

O U T F I E L D E R
F I R S T   B A S E M A N

PITTSBURGH PIRATES 1962-1982

◆　　　◆　　　◆

WILLIE STARGELL was a mainstay of the Pittsburgh Pirates for 21 years. He retired among the all-time leaders in home runs, slugging average, and RBI, and was elected to the Hall of Fame in 1988.

Wilver Dornel Stargell (born in 1940) of Alameda, California, was the middle linebacker on his high school football team. He was signed by the Pirates in 1959. In 1962, Stargell hit 27 home runs in the International League, and was called up to Pittsburgh for good.

Stargell took over left field for the Bucs in '63 and hit .243 with 11 homers. Playing half his games in Forbes Field hurt his power stats, but he started a string of 13 straight 20-homer seasons in 1964. He retired in 1982 with a .282 career average and 475 round-trippers, and is the only man to hit two balls clear out of Dodger Stadium.

> *"If I'm hitting, I can hit anyone. If not, my 12-year-old son can get me out."*
>
> —WILLIE STARGELL

Only in the 1970s, after the Pirates moved to Three Rivers Stadium, did Willie get his due. In 1971, the Pirates won the NL pennant, and Willie led the league with 48 homers. He scored 104 runs and knocked in 125. The Bucs won six NL East titles during the 1970s, and Stargell's 269 homers were the highest total of the decade. Injuries forced a move to first base, and from 1974 to '77, his home run totals declined. In 1978, however, "Pops" came back to bat .295 with 28 homers and 97 RBI.

In 1979, Stargell led the Bucs to the world championship. Though he played in just 126 games, he hit .281 with 32 home runs, and then batted over .400 with five homers in the playoffs and Series. He tied with Keith Hernandez in the voting for the NL MVP Award, and captured the NLCS and World Series MVPs. Honored both for his leadership and his production, he encouraged the Pirates' "Fam-i-lee" by example and in spirit.

MAJOR LEAGUE TOTALS									
BA	G	AB	R	H	2B	3B	HR	RBI	SB
.282	2,360	7,927	1,195	2,232	423	55	475	1,540	17

SAM
THOMPSON

O U T F I E L D E R

DETROIT WOLVERINES 1885-1888
PHILADELPHIA QUAKERS (PHILLIES) 1889-1898
DETROIT TIGERS 1906

◆   ◆   ◆

SAMUEL LUTHER THOMPSON (1860-1922) was a 24-year-old carpenter in his hometown of Danville, Indiana, when a scout for the Evansville club in the Northwest League bade him to give professional baseball a try. Thompson agreed, believing that the $2.50 per game deal was equitable, and ended up in the Hall of Fame.

Joining the NL's Detroit Wolverines in July 1885, Thompson tallied 11 hits in his first 26 at bats and claimed the club's right field job. He led Detroit in batting in 1886, his first full campaign in the majors. In 1887, he paced the entire NL, hitting .372, and bagged a 19th century-record 166 RBI. Still, Thompson's talents went largely unrecognized in his time (RBI totals were not an official statistic). As a result, it was only after Thompson retired that historians revealed him to be the most prolific of any player ever at driving in runs—.921 per game. The home run, another Thompson specialty, was regarded as a trivial accomplishment in the late 1800s, but his lifetime total of 127 home runs was the second-highest tally of the 1876-1892 era.

In 1887, playing in 127 games, Thompson set a major-league single-season record by totaling 166 RBI.

Thompson, however, was not merely a slugger. He also led the NL on three occasions in hits, twice in doubles, and once in triples. A good outfielder, he had one of the strongest arms in the game. The Detroit Wolverines collapsed after the 1888 season, and Sam was sold to the Phillies.

In the early 1890s, Big Sam was joined by Ed Delahanty and Billy Hamilton, giving Philadelphia a trio of future Hall of Fame outfielders. While Hamilton batted .399 in 1894, the other two topped the .400 mark that year. The following year, Thompson hit .392 and led the National League with 18 homers and 165 RBI.

Thompson was the only player to average more than two home runs per every 100 at bats prior to 1900.

A bad back shelved Thompson early in 1897, and despite several comeback attempts, his career was for all intents and purposes finished. In 1906, at age 46, he appeared in eight games with Detroit, playing in the outfield with a 19-year-old rookie named Ty Cobb.

MAJOR LEAGUE TOTALS									
BA	G	AB	R	H	2B	3B	HR	RBI	SB
.331	1,410	6,005	1,263	1,986	340	160	128	1,299	221

ARKY VAUGHAN

SHORTSTOP

PITTSBURGH PIRATES 1932-1941
BROOKLYN DODGERS 1942-1943; 1947-1948

◆ ◆ ◆

A NINE-TIME All-Star, Arky Vaughan was one of the greatest offensive shortstops in baseball history. He led the National League three times each in walks, triples, runs scored, and on-base percentage. Vaughan also paced the league in putouts and assists three times each.

Born in Clifton, Arkansas, Joseph Floyd Vaughan (1912-1952) was raised in Fullerton, California. After playing semi-pro ball, he was signed in 1931 by Wichita of the Western Association, where he hit .338 with 21 homers and 145 runs scored. The Pirates made Arky their starting shortstop in 1932.

In 1935, he hit .385 to lead the National League, slugged 19 home runs, and drove in 99. An outstanding contact hitter, he walked 118 times in 1936 while fanning just 21. He never totaled more than 38 strikeouts in a season. In the 1941 All-Star game, Vaughan became the first player to hit two home runs in a midsummer classic. That season, he led the NL in runs scored and triples while batting .300.

When Vaughan retired in 1948, he held the record for the highest career on-base percentage by a shortstop, garnering a .406 on-base average.

After 10 seasons in Pittsburgh, Vaughan was dealt to the Dodgers, as the Pirates attempted to rebuild the franchise with youth. In 1943, he led the National League in runs scored and stolen bases. However, the mild-mannered Vaughan could not abide Brooklyn manager Leo Durocher. When the Dodgers would not trade him,

Vaughan retired at age 31. He missed the next three seasons, returning only in 1947 when Durocher was suspended for the year. He hit .325 off the bench and saw action in his first World Series. The Yankees, however, bested the Dodgers in seven. After slumping to .244 in 1948, he retired for good. Had he not missed those prime years, Vaughan might have approached 3,000 career hits. Vaughan retired with a .318 career average, the second highest ever by a shortstop.

In 1952, Vaughan drowned in a fishing mishap near Eagleville, California. The Hall of Fame Veterans Committee passed over Vaughan several times before he was selected in 1985.

MAJOR LEAGUE TOTALS									
AB	G	AB	R	H	2B	3B	HR	RBI	SB
.318	1,817	6,622	1,173	2,103	356	128	96	926	118

HONUS WAGNER

INFIELDER
OUTFIELDER

LOUISVILLE COLONELS 1897-1899
PITTSBURGH PIRATES 1900-1917

◆   ◆   ◆

GROWING UP IN A SMALL Pennsylvania German community, John Peter Wagner (1874-1955) was more commonly known as Johannes or Hans. Once he became a baseball player of considerable ability, Hans gave way to Honus.

Wagner was a rarity, the son of an immigrant father who thought baseball was an acceptable profession. Honus began his major-league career with the Louisville Colonels of the National League, batting .321 over three seasons (1897 to 1899) while playing multiple positions. When Louisville disbanded, Wagner joined the Pittsburgh Pirates. Player-manager Fred Clarke used Wagner mainly in the outfield in 1900 and was rewarded when Honus won the first of his record eight National League batting titles and also led the loop in doubles, triples, and slugging average.

When Bones Ely slumped to .208 in 1901, Wagner spelled him for nearly half the season at shortstop. It was the first time Honus had played the position in the majors. In 1902, he was returned to the outfield as the Pirates won the pennant by a record 27½ games. The team was so strong that it could survive several defections to the American League and still triumph for a third successive season in 1903.

Since Wagner's retirement as a player in 1917, his name has appeared in the shortstop slot on almost everyone's all-time All-Star team. Some go even further and rate him the greatest player ever.

Even in his time, Wagner was regarded as a folk hero. A model of clean living, he once had a baseball card of him removed from circulation because it was distributed in cigarette packs. The few copies of the card that survive are now each worth more than the total amount of salary Wagner made during his career. Oddly, a later baseball card of Honus, made when he was a Pittsburgh coach, shows him preparing to ingest a wad of chewing tobacco.

"I name Wagner first on my list, not only because he was . . . baseball's foremost shortstop, but because Honus could have been first at any other position. . . . I never saw such a versatile player."

—John McGraw

There is nothing paradoxical, though, about Wagner's performance on the playing field. He was so great a shortstop that contemporary players must have considered it a cruel act of providence that he was also blessed with such incredible talent as a hitter. During his 21-year career, Wagner was a league leader at least twice in every major offensive department except home runs and walks. When he retired he had compiled more hits, runs, total bases, RBI, and stolen bases than any player in history to that point.

Honus was among the elite group of five players named to the Hall of Fame in 1936 when the first vote for enshrinement was conducted. For some 15 years afterward, he continued to serve as a Pirates coach, a job he had first begun on a regular basis in 1933. Wagner died on December 6, 1955, in Carnegie, Pennsylvania, the town where he was born.

MAJOR LEAGUE TOTALS									
BA	G	AB	R	H	2B	3B	HR	RBI	SB
.327	2,789	10,441	1,735	3,418	643	252	101	1,732	722

ED WALSH

P I T C H E R

CHICAGO WHITE SOX 1904-1916
BOSTON BRAVES 1917

◆　　　◆　　　◆

ORIGINALLY, Edward Augustine Walsh (1881-1959) had an overpowering fastball and little else. In 1904, however, he learned the spitball from White Sox teammate Elmer Stricklett, reputedly the first to master the pitch. Of Walsh's spitter, Sam Crawford once said, "I think the ball disintegrated on the way to the plate and the catcher put it back together again."

Walsh led the AL with 10 shutouts in 1906, and in 1907 won 24 games, worked 422 innings, and collected a pitchers' all-time record 227 assists. The following year, Big Ed labored an American League record 464 innings, hurled 42 complete games, and became the last big-league pitcher to notch 40 victories in a season. Unfortunately, the weak-hitting White Sox still finished third. That October 2, Walsh ceded Cleveland just one run and fanned 15 batters but lost 1-0 when Addie Joss threw a perfect game.

"I think that the ball disintegrated on the way to the plate, and the catcher put it back together again. I swear, when it went past the plate, it was just the spit that went by."

—SAM CRAWFORD ON ED WALSH'S SPITTER

That game was typical of Walsh's fate during his 13 years with the White Sox. Two years later, when he led the AL with a magnificent 1.26 ERA, he nonetheless had a losing record (18-20) as the Sox hit just .211 for the season.

Despite little offensive support, Walsh never lacked for confidence. Charles Dryden called him the only man who "could strut while standing still." Ring Lardner made Big Ed his model for Jack Keefe, the cocky hero of *You Know Me, Al: A Busher's Letters*, the classic work of baseball fiction of the era.

In 1908, Walsh won 40 games, setting a record by winning 44.5 percent of his team's games, as the White Sox garnered 88 wins.

Playing for the penurious Charlie Comiskey, Walsh was forced to work many innings for meager pay. By 1913, this overwork had taken its toll, and he won only 13 games in his last five seasons. He ended his career with "just" 195 wins, but more than compensated with a 1.82 career ERA—the lowest of all time.

MAJOR LEAGUE TOTALS									
W	L	ERA	G	CG	IP	H	ER	BB	SO
195	126	1.82	430	250	2,964.1	2,346	598	617	1,736

PAUL WANER

O U T F I E L D E R

PITTSBURGH PIRATES 1926-1940
BROOKLYN DODGERS 1941; 1943-1944
BOSTON BRAVES 1941-1942
NEW YORK YANKEES 1944-1945

◆   ◆   ◆

PAUL GLEE WANER (1903-1965) left
East Central Teachers College in
Oklahoma against his father's advice to
pursue a professional baseball career in
1923. Signed by Dick Williams of the San
Francisco Seals, Waner never looked
back. Originally a pitcher, he switched to
the outfield after suffering an arm injury in
the Pacific Coast League. With the Seals in
1925, Waner paced the PCL with a .401
batting average and 75 doubles.

Sold to Pittsburgh that winter, Paul
immediately began to demonstrate that he
was cheap even at the high price the Bucs
paid for him. In 1926, his rookie season, he
hit .336, second best in the National

League. "Big Poison" Paul's performance spurred the Pirates to buy his younger brother Lloyd, who became "Little Poison." The two combined to amass a sibling-record 460 hits and bring the Pirates a National League pennant in 1927. That year, Paul led the NL with a .380 average, 237 hits, 17 triples, and 131 RBI to win the MVP Award.

> *"[Waner] said he just laid the bat on his shoulder, and when he saw a pitch he liked, he threw it off."*
> —BUDDY HASSETT

Paul developed into one of the finest hitters in National League history. He won three hitting titles and led the NL at one time or another in every major batting department except home runs and walks. En route to accumulating 3,152 career hits, he set an NL record by tabulating 200 or more hits in a season eight separate times. His 191 triples are the 10th-best total of all time, and in 1932 Paul hit 62 doubles. Waner usually walked 70 times in a season, and finished his career with a .333 average. He was an outstanding fly-catcher, combining a center fielder's speed with a powerful arm.

> *"I saw a lot of good hitters, but I never saw a better one than Paul Waner."*
>
> —BURLEIGH GRIMES

Waner closed out his career with Brooklyn and the Boston Braves and was named to the Hall of Fame in 1952. He returned to the game in 1957 as a batting instructor with the Milwaukee Braves. Later he served in a similar capacity with the Cardinals and the Phillies. A great hitter who could also teach hitting skills, Waner wrote a well-received book on the subject in the early 1960s.

MAJOR LEAGUE TOTALS									
BA	G	AB	R	H	2B	3B	HR	RBI	SB
.333	2,549	9,459	1,626	3,152	603	190	112	1,309	104

HOYT WILHELM

PITCHER

NEW YORK GIANTS 1952-1956
ST. LOUIS CARDINALS 1957
CLEVELAND INDIANS 1957-1958
BALTIMORE ORIOLES 1958-1962
CHICAGO WHITE SOX 1963-1968
CALIFORNIA ANGELS 1969
ATLANTA BRAVES 1969-1970; 1971
CHICAGO CUBS 1970
LOS ANGELES DODGERS 1971-1972

◆   ◆   ◆

HOYT WILHELM BLAZED the trail for the modern relief specialist, and was the first career reliever to enter the Hall of Fame. He entered more games than any pitcher ever, and retired with more relief wins than anyone else.

James Hoyt Wilhelm (born in 1923) grew up in North Carolina as a fan of Washington Senators pitcher Dutch Leonard, one of the first hurlers to rely almost exclusively on the knuckleball. Eventually, Wilhelm himself became a master of the elusive pitch.

A recipient of the Purple Heart in World War II, Wilhelm was a starting pitcher in the minors. He spent eight seasons in the bushes, lost three more years to the war, and did not make his big-league debut until he was 28.

In 1952, Hoyt made the Giants as a reliever, bursting out of nowhere to lead the National League with 71 games pitched, 15 relief wins, and a 2.43 ERA. He led the league in appearances in 1953, and notched 15 saves. In 1954, Wilhelm posted a 2.10 ERA and a league-best 12 relief wins as the Giants won the World Series.

Soon, however, he lost favor with the Giants. The Orioles converted him back to the starting rotation in 1958. Wilhelm promptly tossed a no-hitter that year and then led the AL in 1959 with a 2.19 ERA. Ultimately, he ended up back in the bullpen.

From 1962 to '68, with the Orioles and the White Sox, he registered ERAs below 2.00 six of the seven years. The ageless Wilhelm rolled on, pitching effectively through the early 1970s, and finished his career at age 49 with the 1972 Dodgers. He totaled 227 career saves, including a personal-best 27 in 1964 with the Sox.

Wilhelm hit a home run in his first major-league at bat, in 1952, and then played 21 seasons without hitting another four-bagger.

Like those of other baseball pioneers, many of Wilhelm's career totals have been eclipsed. His total of 1,070 career games still stands. Even if that mark, too, is broken, Wilhelm's place in history—and in the Hall of Fame—is secure.

			MAJOR LEAGUE TOTALS						
W	L	ERA	G	SV	IP	H	ER	BB	SO
143	122	2.52	1,070	227	2,254.0	1,757	632	778	1,610

TED WILLIAMS

OUTFIELDER

BOSTON RED SOX 1939-1942; 1946-1960

◆　　　◆　　　◆

TED WILLIAMS ONCE SAID that he had a dream of walking down the street and having people point to him and saying, "There goes Ted Williams, the greatest hitter who ever lived." Some baseball historians make that claim, with his competition being Babe Ruth. Williams holds the distinction of working harder at hitting than anyone.

Born in 1918 in San Diego, Theodore Samuel Williams spent most of his solitary, difficult childhood playing baseball on the sandlots. Signed by the Red Sox, the brash, young Williams in the 1938 spring training alienated the veteran BoSox outfielders. When Ted was sent down to Minneapolis, he responded, "Tell them I'm going to make more money in this game than all three of them put together." He then won the American Association Triple Crown with a .366 average, 43 homers, and 142 RBI.

Williams made an immediate impact in Boston. He finished his rookie 1939 season with a .327 average, 31 homers, and a league-leading 145 RBI. He led the AL with 134 runs scored while batting .344 in 1940. In 1941 he hit .406, making him the last man to hit over .400. Going into the last day of the year, he was at .39955. Manager Joe Cronin gave Ted the opportunity to sit out the double-header to save his average, which would have rounded up to .400, but Williams played both games and went 6-for-8 to raise his mark to .406. In 1942, Williams produced his first major-league Triple Crown, with a .356 average, 36 home runs, and 137 RBI, yet lost out on the MVP to Joe Gordon.

Williams spent three years as a pilot in World War II, returning in 1946 to lead Boston to his only pennant, winning his first MVP Award. That year he first encountered "The Williams Shift," a defensive scheme invented by Indian manager Lou Boudreau that loaded the defense against Williams pulling the ball, forcing him to hit the other way. Teddy Ballgame captured his second Triple Crown in 1947 (with a .343 batting average, 32 home runs, and 114 RBI) but was denied the MVP, losing to Joe DiMaggio. Ted won the batting crown in 1948 (.369 average) and another MVP in 1949, hitting .343 with a league-leading 43 homers, 159 RBI, 150 runs, and 162 walks.

In 1952, when Ted was 34 years old, he was recalled for the Korean War, where he flew 39 missions, missing most of two more seasons. Back from Korea, he missed out on two more batting titles in 1954 and 1955 because requirements for the league crown counted at bats and not plate appearances. He got two more batting crowns when he hit .388 (with 38 homers) in 1957 when he was 39 years old, and .328 in '58 at age 40. In his last season, 1960, Williams batted .316 with 29 home runs, including one in his last at bat.

> *"Baseball is the only field of endeavor where a man can succeed three times out of 10 and be considered a good performer."*
>
> —TED WILLIAMS

Despite missing five years to military duty, his career numbers are astounding: the highest on-base average in history at .483; the second-highest slugging average at .634; the second-highest number of walks at 2,019; and 521 home runs. Hitting was a science to Williams, who wrote a highly regarded book on the subject. The "Thumper" was elected to the Hall of Fame in 1966. He managed the Washington Senators from 1969 to 1974.

				MAJOR LEAGUE TOTALS					
BA	G	AB	R	H	2B	3B	HR	RBI	SB
.344	2,292	7,706	1,798	2,654	525	71	521	1,839	24

DAVE WINFIELD

O U T F I E L D E R

SAN DIEGO PADRES 1973-1980
NEW YORK YANKEES 1981-1990
CALIFORNIA ANGELS 1990-1991
TORONTO BLUE JAYS 1992
MINNESOTA TWINS 1993-1994
CLEVELAND INDIANS 1995

◆   ◆   ◆

BORN IN ST. PAUL, MINNESOTA, in 1951, David Mark Winfield was an amazing athlete. He was drafted by the Orioles, but chose to attend the University of Minnesota, where he played baseball and basketball. In 1973, Winfield was the Padres' first-round draft pick. In addition, he was also drafted by football's Minnesota Vikings, the NBA's Atlanta Hawks, and the ABA's New Orleans Jazz.

Winfield signed with the Padres, skipping the minors entirely and landing in the

Padres' outfield. Dave broke loose in 1977 with 25 homers and 92 RBI. He hit .300 each of the next two years, with 58 total homers and 215 total RBI. His fielding improved, and he earned his first of seven Gold Gloves in 1979. Winfield also showed a tremendous throwing arm.

> *"But internally, for a guy to be successful, you have to be like a clock spring—wound but loose at the same time."*
>
> —DAVE WINFIELD

After the 1980 season, Winfield elected free agency and signed with the Yankees. He became baseball's highest-paid player at that time. In New York, he was successful on the field and controversial out of uniform. Winfield's 1988 autobiography offered unbridled criticism of Yankee owner George Steinbrenner, who himself called Winfield "Mr. May," in reference to Dave's supposed inability to hit like "Mr. October," Reggie Jackson, in the clutch.

A 12-time All-Star, Winfield hit 37 dingers in 1982 and 32 in 1983. Between 1982 and '89, his lowest RBI total was 97. He sat out the 1989 season with a herniated disk, but returned at age 38 in 1990 to hit 21 homers. In 1992, he collected 108 RBI and helped the Blue Jays win the world championship.

Although Winfield led his league in a major offensive category just once (pacing the NL with 118 RBI in 1979), he was an exciting, explosive player in his early years and a consistent power threat as his career progressed. In 1993, Winfield was signed by his hometown Twins, and collected his 3,000th hit that September at the Metrodome. After an injury-plagued stint with the 1995 Indians, Winfield called it quits after amassing 3,110 hits and 465 career homers.

MAJOR LEAGUE TOTALS									
BA	G	AB	R	H	2B	3B	HR	RBI	SB
.283	2,973	11,003	1,669	3,110	540	88	465	1,833	233

CARL
YASTRZEMSKI
OUTFIELDER
FIRST BASEMAN

BOSTON RED SOX 1961-1983

❖   ❖   ❖

A GREAT HITTER FOR SEVERAL seasons and a very good hitter for many more, Carl Yastrzemski performed the impossible—replacing Ted Williams—well enough to make the Hall of Fame.

Carl Michael Yastrzemski (born in 1939) of Southampton, New York, was pursued by several pro teams, but spurned them to attend Notre Dame in 1958. After one year, he turned professional and signed with the Red Sox. In 1959, he led the Carolina League with a .377 batting average, and in 1960 paced the American Association with 193 hits.

Williams retired after 1960, and Yaz took his left field spot. He batted .266 in his first season and improved to .296 with 94 RBI in 1962. Carl won his first batting title in 1963 at .321, and showed power and patience. He ultimately walked over 100 times in six seasons.

"Ed, you're the second-best umpire in the league. The other 23 are tied for first."

—CARL YASTRZEMSKI TO UMPIRE ED RUNGE

In 1965, Yastrzemski led the AL with a .536 slugging percentage and 45 doubles, and in 1966 led the circuit with 39 doubles. The Red Sox, a ninth-place team in 1966, won the pennant on the last day of a wild 1967 season. Yaz, hitting .326 with a career-best 44 homers, became the last man to win a Triple Crown by hitting .522 in the final two weeks of the season and was named the AL MVP. In the World Series he hit .400, but the Sox lost in seven.

Carl won another batting title in 1968, and hit 40 homers in both 1969 and 1970.

Ted Williams said that Yaz "reminded me of myself at that age . . . he positively quivered waiting for that next pitch." Yaz swung a big bat for 23 seasons and patrolled left field expertly for the Red Sox.

Yastrzemski collected his 3,000th hit in 1979 and retired in 1983 with 452 homers and a .285 average. He was the first American League player with 3,000 hits and 400 home runs. Cooperstown called his name in 1989.

MAJOR LEAGUE TOTALS

BA	G	AB	R	H	2B	3B	HR	RBI	SB
.285	3,308	11,988	1,816	3,419	646	59	452	1,844	168

CY YOUNG
PITCHER

CLEVELAND SPIDERS 1890-1898
ST. LOUIS PERFECTOS (CARDINALS) 1899-1900
BOSTON SOMERSETS (PILGRIMS, RED SOX)
1901-1908; 1911
CLEVELAND NAPS 1909-1911

◆　　　◆　　　◆

U PON BEING SIGNED by Canton of the Tri-State League in 1890, the 23-year-old Young was seen warming up against a wooden fence. The ensuing damage to the barrier was likened to that of a cyclone hitting a wall. A sportswriter shortened "cyclone" to "Cy."

Denton True Young (1867-1955) joined the Cleveland Spiders later that year. Cap Anson, player-manager of the Chicago White Stockings, rejected Young earlier that year as being "just another big farmer." After Cy beat Chicago in his first major-league outing, Anson tried in vain to purchase him.

Throughout the 1890s, Young was the top pitcher in the game, blending stamina, guile, and excellent control. During the '90s, he registered 267 victories with a high of 36. However, when attendance sagged in Cleveland, Young and most of the team's other stars were shipped to St. Louis in 1899.

"A pitcher's got to be good and he's got to be lucky to get a no-hit game."
—CY YOUNG

Turning 33 in 1900, Young registered just 19 wins, his lowest output since his rookie season. Cy then signed with Boston in the new American League. Rumors of Young's decline were dispelled as he led the yearling major league in wins in 1901, then repeated his feat the next two years.

Cy won 20 or more games six times for the Boston Americans and participated in the first modern World Series in 1903. Perhaps the finest effort of his career came on May 5, 1904, when he pitched a perfect game against Rube Waddell and the Philadelphia Athletics.

"I won more games than you ever saw."

—Cy Young to a reporter

Young retired in 1911 with 511 career victories, 7,357 innings pitched, and no sore arm. Cy was inducted into the Hall of Fame in 1938. Shortly after Young's death, Commissioner Ford Frick originated the Cy Young Award, an annual honor bestowed upon the pitcher deemed most valuable in each league.

MAJOR LEAGUE TOTALS									
W	L	ERA	G	CG	IP	H	ER	BB	SO
511	315	2.63	906	750	7,356.0	7,092	2,147	1,217	2,796